Oneselves

T0055160

ALSO BY LOUIS BALDWIN
AND FROM MCFARLAND

*Portraits of God: Word Pictures of the Deity from
the Earliest Times Through Today* (1986; paperback 2012)

*Turning Points: Pivotal Moments in the
Careers of 83 Famous Figures* (1999)

*Women of Strength: Biographies of 106 Who Have Excelled
in Traditionally Male Fields, A.D. 61 to the Present* (1996)

Oneselves

Multiple Personalities, 1811–1981

LOUIS BALDWIN

McFarland & Company, Inc., Publishers
Jefferson, North Carolina, and London

To Virginia

The present work is a reprint of the library bound edition of
Oneselves: Multiple Personalities, 1811–1981, *first published*
in 1984 by McFarland.

LIBRARY OF CONGRESS CATALOGUING-IN-PUBLICATION DATA

Baldwin, Louis.
    Oneselves : multiple personalities, 1811–1981 / Louis Baldwin.
        p.   cm.
    Includes bibliographical references and index.

    ISBN 978-0-7864-6719-8
    softcover : acid free paper ∞

    1. Multiple personality.   I. Title.
    RC569.5.M8B35 2012
    616.85'236   84-42603

BRITISH LIBRARY CATALOGUING DATA ARE AVAILABLE

© 1984 Louis Baldwin. All rights reserved

No part of this book may be reproduced or transmitted in any form
or by any means, electronic or mechanical, including photocopying
or recording, or by any information storage and retrieval system,
without permission in writing from the publisher.

Front cover design by David K. Landis (Shake It Loose Graphics)

Manufactured in the United States of America

McFarland & Company, Inc., Publishers
* Box 611, Jefferson, North Carolina 28640*
* www.mcfarlandpub.com*

Contents

Foreword

There are more things in the human mind and heart, a twentieth-century Hamlet might remark, than are dreamt of in our psychology. Among these things are the nature of human personality, the continuity of the "self," the process of memory, the disintegration of behavior patterns under the influence of hallucinogens. Among them also are familiar examples of alcoholic amnesia, delightfully illustrated by Charlie Chaplin's *City Lights*, in which the little tramp is alternately befriended, and then rejected, by an alternately drunk, and then sober, millionaire. And among them especially are the phenomena of multiple personality, about which a typical word used by psychiatrists is "baffling."

Another frequently used word is "nonsense." Perhaps half of the psychiatrists in the United States either dismiss the notion of multiple personality outright or view it with various degrees of Missouri-brand skepticism. Another third or so seem relatively open-minded about it, receptive but hesitant. And about a fifth accept it as a separate, recognizable and specifically treatable mental and emotional disorder. In general, these also are the psychiatrists who use hypnosis as a therapeutic tool. The correlation is reasonable, since the hypnotic state often resembles the multiple-personality pathology. Indeed, a leading American hypnotherapist, Ernest Hilgard, maintains that the hypnotic state characteristically includes a "hidden observer," subliminal but accessible to the hypnotherapist, and displaying a relatively rational, objective attitude.

The professional bias against diagnoses of multiple personality is weakening. A century ago the bias was in the other direction. In 1911, however, a Swiss neurologist, Paul Eugen Bleuler, offered the label *schizophrenia* to replace the rather awkward and misleading term *dementia praecox*. The new label caught on, becoming dominant during the next couple of decades in diagnosing cases of "split personality."

Bleuler himself recognized that the splitting involved in the psychosis of schizophrenia is far more extreme than that observed in the hysterical neurosis of multiple personality. (The departure from reality and the inability to function rationally also are much more pronounced.) The similarity of symptoms, however, tended to obscure this distinction in most diagnoses. Further, the rise of Pavlovian behaviorism, especially a la B.F. Skinner, encouraged disdain for any untidy, nonmechanistic views of human abnormalities. As a result, the number of cases of multiple personality reported in *Psychological Abstracts* and listed in *Index Medicus* began dropping in the 1920s and virtually disappeared in the 1950s and '60s. Yet in the mid-fifties, with the publication of the best-selling *The Three Faces of Eve* and the release of the popular movie based on that book, the seeds of revival were already beginning to sprout. In the 1970s, which saw the appearance of the similarly best-selling book *Sybil* and the television drama based on it, more than fifty cases of multiple personality were reported, as against ninety in the preceding century and a half.

These figures are approximate, depending on how the term is defined. Only in 1980 did the American Psychiatric Association, in the third edition of its *Diagnostic and Statistical Manual of Psychiatric Disorders*, define multiple personality as a distinct disorder and establish criteria for diagnosis. At any given time, it specified, the patient's consciousness is dominated by one of two or more distinguishable personalities, with that personality controlling behavior; in addition, each personality is complicated (with its own set of memories, characteristics, etc.), and changes of personality are abrupt. Amnesia was mentioned as a usual concomitant, although most hypnotherapists would probably include it as an essential ingredient. The definition is likely to be only a precursor of more refined and sophisticated definitions to come.

The growing sophistication in the diagnosis, treatment, and indeed the reporting of cases of multiple personality is readily discernible in the more than two dozen cases described in the following pages, since they run the gamut from the early days, when multiple personality was barely emerging from the dark recesses of demonic possession, to the present, when a patient's various personalities are often analyzed through psychological testing. Some of the early cases would no longer be classified as instances of multiple personality by some of today's authorities, although the resemblances are generally more striking than the differences. Persistent time loss, chronic sleepwalking, automatic writing, hallucination and multiple personality are all closely associated.

Classification may be a science, but it is an arbitrary one. These cases illustrate the great variety of possible causes and effects, of symptoms and cures, which the still "baffled" psychiatric profession must organize into a coherent phenomenology. It does seem to be bracing itself for just such a project.

> *It should be noted that subjects' identities have been disguised throughout, for obvious reasons, except when the individuals have made themselves known or have become known through media publicity.*

"With every day, and from both sides of my intelligence, the moral and the intellectual, I thus drew steadily nearer to that truth, by whose partial discovery I have been doomed to such a terrible shipwreck: that man is not truly one, but truly two. I say two, because the state of my own knowledge does not pass beyond that point. Others will follow, others will outstrip me on the same lines; and I hazard the guess that man will ultimately be known for a mere polity of multifarious, incongruous, and independent denizens."

 —Dr. Henry Jekyll (Robert Louis Stevenson)

Was it Hamlet wronged Laertes? Never Hamlet:
If Hamlet from himself be ta'en away,
And when he's not himself does wrong Laertes,
Then Hamlet does it not, Hamlet denies it.
Who does it, then? His madness: if 't be so,
Hamlet is of the faction that is wronged;
His madness is poor Hamlet's enemy.
 —Act V, Scene 2

Mary Reynolds, 1811

The case of Mary Reynolds seems to be the earliest case of multiple personality ever reported. William James, in his *Principles of Psychology* (Holt, 1890), gave a rather detailed account of it, with a bow to the original chronicler, a Dr. Weir Mitchell.

This "dull and melancholy young woman," as James described her, lived with her family in the backwoods of Pennsylvania. One morning in 1811, when she was about eighteen, she failed to get up at her usual time. Members of her family went to her room to awaken her but could not do so. Some ten hours later, in the evening, she finally awoke, but in an extraordinary state of mind. Indeed, "state of mind" may not be a very apt phrase for describing her condition, since it was precisely her mind that seemed to be missing, or at least her memory. She did not recognize any of her family or friends, her room, the house, or the surrounding countryside. She had a vocabulary of a few elementary words, but they clearly had no meaning for her. Her body in both structure and function was that of an eighteen-year-old woman, but her mind gave every indication of having returned to infancy. Again it was chiefly her lack of memory that suggested this; some other aspects of her mind, such as her ability to appreciate the beauties of nature, seemed relatively unimpaired.

Although such a phenomenon must have been unprecedented in their experience, her family and friends seem to have taken her unusual condition in their stride, reacting with a backwoods equanimity that probably could not have been expected of their more highly strung city cousins. Their first efforts were devoted to introducing themselves, but the results were thoroughly disappointing. The new personality—we may as well call her May for convenience—not only was hard to communicate with but also adamantly refused to acknowledge any relationships, like someone who had suddenly found herself unaccountably translated into a foreign and probably hostile environment. She had

1

some sort of guard up, and they couldn't penetrate it. Yet she was otherwise very amiable and cooperative.

Next they tried teaching her to read and write, with much greater success. The writing started off a bit awkwardly: when her brother wrote out her name for her to copy, she did so backwards, from right to left, and it took her a while to overcome this curiously Oriental predisposition. But she was consistently receptive and eager to learn. Her mind was not quite the *tabula rasa* it seemed, for she absorbed the necessary information and skill forty or fifty times as fast as a normal young child might have. Within a few weeks she could read and write as well as her teachers.

This achievement may have resulted partly from her disposition, for May was anything but "dull and melancholy." Unlike Mary, she was cheerful rather than lugubrious, gregarious rather than withdrawn, talkative rather than reticent, vigorous rather than languid. She was much more appreciative of the works of nature all around her, the hills and dales, the woods and meadows, the fields and streams. She loved wandering about the countryside, quite aimlessly, regularly walking or riding away early in the morning and not returning until quite late at night. She may have enjoyed human company, but obviously she didn't need it.

The country in that part of Pennsylvania was a wilderness, replete with such delights as bears, panthers, and poisonous snakes. Reacting to the inevitable warnings with good-natured contempt, she revealed a peculiar delusion about which she evidently was quite sincere. She often saw bears in the forest, she told her friends, or rather what they called bears. Actually, she explained, they weren't bears at all, but only large, black hogs. Completely harmless.

Apparently May never got rid of this delusion, which, on at least one occasion if her story was true, resulted in her living somewhat dangerously. Returning one evening from one of her sojourns in the country, what she described as "a great black hog" suddenly confronted her as she was riding through the woods. When she reined her horse to a stop, the hog rose upright on its rear legs and "impudently" grimaced at her, gnashing its teeth. She began urging the horse forward, but the hog stayed in their path, and the horse flatly refused to budge. She tried the whip, but her valiant steed in response began trying to turn and go back. Frustrated by the horse, she turned her attention to the hog, demanding loudly that it get out of their way, but it proved equally recalcitrant. With her impatience coming to a boil, she dismounted, picked up a stick, and angrily bore down upon her adversary. At her approach the hog lost its impudence and, dropping to all fours, turned and grumpily stalked away, glancing back now and then for a departing growl. Triumphantly May and her horse continued on their way. Doubtless Mary would have died on the spot.

And so things went until, about five weeks after May had abruptly arrived, she as abruptly departed. One morning, after a longer sleep than usual, Mary woke up and greeted her parents and brothers and sisters as though nothing at all unusual had happened since she had last gone to sleep. That was the way it seemed to her, although she was forced to admit that some things certainly had changed much more than could be accounted for by only those few hours. She was completely familiar with the members of her family, and for their part they had to admit (though not necessarily to her) that this was the same dull, melancholy Mary they had always known. Her chronic dejection was, furthermore, considerably aggravated by the stories they had to tell her of the preceding weeks. She busied herself with her old routine of housework and other duties, hoping that her absorption in familiar activities would keep her from falling to pieces again.

But the strategy proved futile. A few weeks later she again dropped off into an abnormally deep sleep and awoke the next morning as May. Her comments and behavior gave every indication that she was completely unaware of the lapse of time. It was a total amnesia, like Mary's; as she understood it, she simply had had a good night's sleep. She was soon disabused of this notion, of course, but, unlike Mary, she accepted the news of her absence with great good humor. In fact, she thought the whole thing was (and the double meaning is intentional) hysterical.

A few weeks later Mary returned, and a few weeks after that May reappeared. And so it went for the next fifteen years or so, until she was about 35 years old, when she went to live with her nephew John, a clergyman, to keep house for him and to help with his parish duties. He may have had some misgivings, but doubtless she was in straitened circumstances, and this was long before government became interested in social security.

If he did have misgivings, they proved unfounded. Soon after the move, her attitudes and behavior began to change, very slowly but quite observably. Her dissociations became less frequent, and the differences between the two personalities became less radical. The two seemed to be merging into one person, a person with characteristics falling somewhere between those of the separate personalities. She was neither melancholy nor boisterously merry, but was pleasantly cheerful. She was neither painfully diffident or exuberantly convivial, but was engagingly affable. She was neither taciturn nor garrulous,but was quietly responsive. She was neither lethargic nor bursting with energy, but was industrious—a quality that served her well as housekeeper. She enjoyed nature without disappearing into it for ten or twelve hours each day. It need hardly be added that her relatives and friends were utterly delighted with what they called her third personality.

She spent the remaining quarter-century of her life with her nephew. One morning in January, 1854, when she was 61 years old, she got up, ate breakfast, and started on her household chores (mostly supervisory now). In the midst of her work she suddenly held her head between her hands, crying out, "Oh, I wonder what's the matter with my head!" and collapsed upon the floor. After being lifted to a sofa, she lay there for a few moments, breathing with difficulty, and then died.

Ansel Bourne, 1887

Ansel Bourne was a very solid citizen of Greene, Rhode Island (1970 population: 100), in the latter part of the nineteenth century. Yet there were a few items in his history suggesting that he might not be quite so solid a personality, items to which no particular significance was attached until his identity problems began. In the disciplines of psychology, as in all others, there's nothing like hindsight.

Throughout his life—he was now in his forties—he had had severe headaches usually associated with periods of depression. As a young man he had been trained and had worked as a carpenter, but in his late twenties he had gone temporarily blind and deaf, for some reason that apparently was not clear at the time or later. Reporting the case in his *Principles of Psychology* (Holt, 1890), William James simply described the event as "a sudden temporary loss of sight and hearing under very peculiar circumstances." Whatever the cause, Bourne gave up carpentry and from then on spent his life primarily as an itinerant preacher. He seems to have settled more or less permanently in the village of Greene in the 1880s, establishing for himself a reputation of self-reliance and honest sobriety. His word was his bond.

And then, one day in mid-January, 1887, he disappeared. He went to his bank in Providence, withdrew $551 (a large sum in those days, but he had been considering the purchase of some property in Greene), paid some bills, and boarded a horse-car bound for Pawtucket. That was the last that his family and friends saw of him for the next eight weeks, and indeed that was the last that Ansel Bourne remembered for the same period.

Early in February one A.J. Brown arrived in Norristown, Pennsylvania. He found a small vacant store, rented it, and stocked it with an inventory of fruit, candies, and small miscellaneous items. For the next six weeks he unobtrusively conducted his business in this not-so-general store, which apparently filled a need and won ready acceptance in the town. None of his customers noticed anything at all unusual about anything he said or did.

5

They did notice something, however, on March 14. Some of his neighbors that morning heard him calling to them in a voice filled with panic. When they rushed to his room he implored them to tell him how he came to be in these strange surroundings. When they addressed him as Mr. Brown, he informed them apprehensively that his name was Ansel Bourne, from Rhode Island. Where in the Lord's name, he asked, was he? Norristown. Norristown, what? Why, Pennsylvania. Oh, Lord, he cried, what was he doing in *Pennsylvania*? But that hardly was a question that they could answer.

Indeed, they now considered him insane, and so did the doctor whom they brought to examine him. The tension was relieved only when, at Bourne's urgent request, they sent a wire to his nephew Andrew Harris, in Providence, and received a reply confirming his real identity. When Harris arrived in Norristown he straightened things out as best he could. After liquidating the stock and vacating the store, which Bourne flatly refused ever to enter again, he took his perplexed uncle back home.

Brown had seemed perfectly normal, his former customers reported: he was rather reticent, minded his own business, and was very orderly and industrious. He had kept his store well stocked, making several trips to Philadelphia for that purpose. He prepared his own meals in the back of the shop, and slept there at night. He attended church regularly and on one occasion had delivered a lay sermon which the congregation had found most inspiring—and in which, it turned out, he recounted a personal experience unwittingly appropriated from the life of Ansel Bourne.

Thus Bourne was able to reconstruct his Brownian activities in Norristown from early February to mid-March through the testimony of others, but he still had no idea at all about what might have happened in those two last, and lost, weeks of January. Since his efforts to discover what he might have done in Pawtucket were futile (he had to assume that he arrived there, for the horse-car company was no help in unraveling the mystery), he couldn't even begin to retrace his route from Pawtucket to Norristown. His frustration over the two lost weeks did nothing for his general stability, and evidently he began seeking psychiatric help.

And so it was that he arrived, with his wife, at James's office one day in June, 1890. In that first interview James, guessing that Bourne would be highly susceptible to hypnotism, suggested that he put the troubled man into a trance in the hope of recalling the secondary personality and the associated memories. Bourne agreed. It took very little effort to get him into the trance, whereupon Brown emerged. James introduced himself—and Mrs. Bourne, whom Brown was sure he had never seen before. The storekeeper seemed to accept James's account of his situation readily enough, although he could recollect nothing from Bourne's life in spite of strong encouragement. His memory of the Norristown episode was so precise, however, that James was inclined to accept his story of the missing fortnight. Actually, nothing very exciting had happened. From Pawtucket he had gone to Boston. He spent the night there, the next night in New York, and the following afternoon in Newark. From there he traveled to Philadelphia, where he spent ten days relaxing, catching up on his reading, and generally making like a vacationer. And then to Norristown.

In the interview with James he was very discouraged. He felt "hedged in," he said; "I can't get out at either end. I don't know what set me down in that Pawtucket horse-car, and I don't know how I left that store, or what became of it." He seemed much less resilient than Bourne, less vigorous, less alert in his responses, yet very similar in other respects.

Ultimately James was discouraged, too. He had hoped to merge the two personalities into one, combining their memories, through a combination of hypnotism and a kind of elementary psychoanalysis. But he failed to make a dent in the man's, or men's, condition. Near the end of his report he had to concede that "Mr. Bourne's skull today still covers two distinct personal selves."

Alma, 1893

Alma's case seems almost to have been one of intelligent, if unconscious, adjustment. The other two personalities in the case were so solicitous and cooperative that they seem deliberately designed for the task of rescue, or at least relief, from an uncomfortable situation.

The case was reported in 1893, in the *Journal of Nervous and Mental Diseases*, by Dr. R.O. Mason, who had been observing Alma's unusual behavior for the preceding ten years. Until her eighteenth year her health had been splendid. She was a superlative athlete, a topflight achiever in school gymnastics and sports. She was also a superlative student, having accumulated not only a spectacular scholastic grade-point average but also an impressive store of formal knowledge. She could read and write Latin, was proficient in mathematics, and was well acquainted with the main currents in the history of philosophy. She had a retentive memory and knew by heart much of the poetry in the Bible, as well as entire poems of her favorite poets, such as Browning, Tennyson and Scott.

But in her eighteenth year she changed. Dr. Mason's report ascribes the change, laconically, to "overwork at school," leaving all details to our imagination. Those details may have been connected with pressures from parents, peers or school authorities, or from within herself. Or she may earlier have suffered an injury, perhaps a head injury, to which no one attached any significance at the time. But whatever the cause, her failing health was clearly observable. Instead of brimming with energy, she now grew weak and listless, and her robust euphoria was replaced by chronic discomfort and persistently recurrent pain.

This change apparently occurred rather gradually, but the next change was quite abrupt. Suddenly she seemed to have emerged from her illness, yet without returning fully to her former state. She obviously felt well, was no longer in pain, and could eat without discomfort. She had recovered most of her strength and nearly all of her old

8

energy. She was lively, alert, cheerful. Indeed, she was bouncy, even childishly so. She exhibited a sprightly intelligence, a perceptive intuition, but none of the effects of Alma's considerable formal education. Her vocabulary, in fact, proved quite limited, her speech rather ungrammatical, and her diction clouded by a "peculiar dialect." (The doctor's report describes the dialect as "decidedly Indian in character" but fails to specify whether east Indian or American Indian is meant.) If the possibility of the emergence of another personality had not by now occurred to Dr. Mason, it surely must have when she identified herself as "Twoey." Although she never spelled the name, she obviously meant it to be a diminutive of "Two"; she always, at this point and henceforward, referred to Alma as "Number One."

As time passed, it became clear that Twoey could come and go as she pleased, whatever Alma's preference, although her appearances usually seemed to be triggered by a worsening of Alma's malaise. Most of her emergences were limited to a few hours, but sometimes she would stay on deck for several days. At the end of each emergence, whatever its length, she would fall into a brief sleep, from which Alma would awake and carry on with whatever she had been doing immediately before *she* had fallen asleep and been replaced by Twoey.

To Alma, Twoey's emergences were blanks, periods of total amnesia. She knew of Twoey's existence and character only from the testimony of relatives and friends. Twoey, however, showed herself to be fully conscious of Alma (as a distinct, completely separate personality inhabiting the body), of her activities, and of at least some of her thoughts. Both personalities were attractive in many respects, and they got along famously, if rather awkwardly. Although they could not communicate directly, Twoey could leave notes for Alma in what passed for a transliteration of her rather opaque dialect. These notes to Alma were most solicitous in telling her what had happened during her absence, giving her information that she might need in resuming her conscious existence, and sometimes offering advice which the doctor described as "always sound and to the point." Friends and relatives were very helpful in establishing and reinforcing this rapport. They were universally delighted with Twoey and were always glad to see her, for they knew that Alma would be feeling better on her return.

Although things could have been much worse, nobody was really satisfied with this as a permanent arrangement, and so the doctor embarked on a course of therapy. Besides "a change of scene and air," it included hypnotism and "the use of animal magnetism," the latter being a very fashionable and sometimes quite effective psychological tool ninety years ago. Whether because or in spite of his treatment, Alma's condition steadily improved until Twoey's visits became quite rare, occasioned only by instances of severe fatigue or mental stress. She grew so well, in fact, that within a couple of years she was married, becoming "a most admirable wife and intelligent and efficient mistress of the household."

Being such a wife and major-domo may have been too great a strain. Before long Twoey began emerging more and more often. The strain may have been too great for her, too, for she suddenly announced one evening that she would now be leaving and would be replaced by a third personality who could do more for Alma in her present circumstances. She then fell unconscious, remaining so for several hours. When she awoke, it was indeed a third personality who greeted those in attendance.

This new personality, though undeniably feminine, unaccountably introduced herself as "The Boy." This anomaly was soon forgotten, however, amid her assurances that she had come to help Alma as much as she possibly could. (To avoid confusion, we'll call her "Three." Apparently she was willing to answer to the name of Alma.) Her assurances proved most reliable. She was on deck for much longer periods than Twoey had ever been—for weeks, in some instances—and, as she accumulated experience, she fully restored Alma's reputation as wife and household mistress. (The doctor's report does not discuss the husband's reaction, but presumably he enjoyed this pseudopolygamy.)

Like Twoey, she lacked Alma's education, but, also like Twoey, she was intelligent and intensely interested in everything going on about her, and so (still like Twoey) she developed a detailed familiarity with family matters, as well as an affectionate intimacy with family members. But unlike Twoey, she accumulated a wealth of information on current events in the world at large, including contemporary literature, music, art and the theater. And, considering her conspicuous lack of background, her critical judgments were considered astonishingly informed and perceptive.

Three was fully and directly aware of both Alma and Twoey. She had enormous respect for Alma's talents and character, and great affection for her; like Twoey, she never emerged except for Alma's benefit. She was equally but not similarly fond of Twoey, for whose more antic disposition she showed admiration heavily laced with loyalty. Some of Twoey's more frolicsome capers, when they came up in reminiscing conversation, usually elicited a good measure of derogatory comment, to which Three steadfastly refused to listen.

There were hints of extrasensory perception in the behavior of all three personalities, but in Three's case this characteristic took a most peculiar form. At times she would become deaf, temporarily but completely deaf, yet during these periods she could understand whatever was said to her apparently by reading lips, although of course neither she nor the other personalities had ever been trained to do so. A more likely explanation might be an unconscious process of selective hearing. But whatever the explanation, her performance must have been impressive. "I myself," Dr. Mason reported, "have seen her sit and attend to the reading of a new book simply by watching the lips of the reader, taking in every word and sentiment, and laughing heartily at the funny passages, when I am perfectly sure she could not have heard a pistol-shot . . . ."

The transitions from one personality to another, the doctor testified, often were beautiful to see. On one occasion he joined Three in a box at the Metropolitan Opera House to hear Beethoven's *Concerto in C Major*, of which Alma was especially fond. During the performance he noticed a change in her facial expression: "a clear, calm, softened look came into the face as she leaned back in her chair and listened to the music with the most intense enjoyment." After it was over, he made a remark to her on the quality of the performance, and she agreed "in the soft and musical tones" which he instantly recognized as Alma's. A few minutes later he saw her close her eyes and take two or three breaths. Her facial expression changed again, and Three commented to him on how nice it was that Alma had been able to emerge long enough to hear her favorite concerto.

This condition of dual personality shared by Alma and Three evidently was the state of the case when the doctor's report was published. The report does not reveal any urgent anxiety on his part to try again to change the situation, perhaps because he was reluctant to risk crossing that invisible line between necessary therapy and unwarranted meddling. A major problem in medicine generally, and today more than ever, has been knowing when to let well enough alone.

Joseph Hoover, 1894

Joseph Hoover was a hardworking, sober, prosperous artisan and businessman. He lived in a small, bustling town near Philadelphia in the latter part of the nineteenth century, where he worked for many years as an expert tinsmith and plumber, building up a thriving business, a sizeable fortune, and a solid reputation. His sons joined the firm upon reaching their majority, contributing a youthful energy and business acumen that increased profits even further.

Now somewhat past middle age, he had always enjoyed good health. His behavior reflected this: there were never any signs of what today we might call neurotic tendencies. He treated his wife and children with love, affection and solicitude. And, in the words of Dr. A.E. Osborne, who reported the case in 1894 in *The Medico-Legal Journal*, "he was not known to have any secret, immoral, or illicit indulgences of any kind whatever."

He disappeared on a bleak, overcast Sunday in November. He had spent the day inside, doing some reading and joining his younger children in some games. Then, sometime around four in the afternoon, he got up from the sofa where he had been reading, put on shoes and a jacket, and started out the front door. His wife called to him that dinner would be ready soon, and he assured her that he was only going out for a breath of fresh air and would be back in a few minutes.

He did not come back in a few minutes, nor in a few hours. Afternoon faded into evening, by which time the family was sufficiently alarmed to resort to the police. Days of investigation yielded not a single clue as to his whereabouts. Although he was well-known throughout the town, no one could recall seeing him any time after he had stepped out of the house. He could not have vanished more completely if he had simply evaporated on the front porch.

After several months of hiring private investigators and publishing offers of rewards for information, the family yielded to despair. Although Hoover had not taken any money and had left the family very well off, they were too disheartened to stay in those familiar surroundings, which reminded them of him continually. After selling their home, the business, and the rest of the family property, they all packed up and moved to Chicago.

About two years later, in a tin-working shop in the Deep South, one of the relatively new workers suddenly put down his work, held his head in his hands, and cried out in alarm and confusion, "My God, where am I? How did I get here? This isn't my shop! Where am I? What does this mean?" At first his fellow workers laughed at these antics—yet tentatively, for they knew him to be a quiet, reserved fellow who wasn't likely to go into an act for purposes of entertainment. But after observing the changes in his facial expression, the beads of sweat gathering on his forehead, and the bewilderment in the questions he was asking them, they grew more sympathetic. Not that they could be of any real help to him—indeed, they perplexed him further by calling him by a name that he had never heard before. Desperately he rushed to the office of the proprietor of the shop, who was no less astonished than the men, and no more informative. All he could offer were some bare facts in confirmation of their story: several months earlier he had hired a man who looked very much like Hoover but did not behave very much like him, even discounting for Hoover's present emotional turmoil. The man had been punctual, diligent, and highly competent. He had kept to himself and had offered no information of any personal nature. In fact, he seemed to have forgotten almost everything about his past, but after all that was his business. The proprietor wasn't the prying sort.

As he listened, Hoover began to develop a hazy recollection of his French leave on that forgotten Sunday of two years before, enough to recognize that what he had undergone was a period of amnesia. After some hasty farewells, he hurried to his lodgings and gathered up his few belongings. He had to borrow some money; curiously, he had saved no money out of his wages, which had been quite substantial. Then he headed for Philadelphia and his home town, where he was given the shocking news of his family's move to Chicago.

The reunion in Chicago was a joyous occasion, and he seems to have lived quite comfortably thereafter. Yet he never got rid of an uneasy feeling that he might be mentally unbalanced. The mystery was never solved. No reasons were ever found for his abrupt departure, for his wandering about the country, for his amnesia. He remained in constant fear that he might do something like that again at any time. But evidently he never did.

Peter Scott, 1894

Peter Scott's dissociation, whatever its cause, was triggered by a leaking gas pipe.

According to Dr. C.L. Dana, who reported the case in 1894 in *The Psychological Review*, he was "an active, intelligent and healthy young man" in his mid-twenties. His family had a history of some "nervousness," but there had never been any symptoms of unusual mental disturbance. He himself had never been seriously ill. His conduct was unremarkable, conforming satisfactorily to the Victorian standards of the time. Although he had been under some stress and strain over the past year or so, due chiefly to some financial problems, he had maintained his good health and, at least ostensibly, his good spirits.

One Saturday morning he failed to show up for the family breakfast. No one in the family felt any particular concern until someone smelled gas and rushed to his bedroom, where he was found still in bed. The room was full of gas from a leak in the pipe, and he was quite unconscious. His eyes were open, his face was flushed, his lips were blue, and he was breathing with great difficulty. The family doctor was called; it took him three hours to restore the breathing to normal. Scott remained unconscious until mid-afternoon, when he began talking to a visiting minister; he seemed rational, but he spoke thickly and not very intelligibly. He did not seem to recognize anyone, even the members of his family.

On the following morning he did recognize his father and his sister. Obviously filled with anxiety, he told them that he was afraid that he might be losing his mind. That afternoon he sank into a state of fitful delirium, and for the rest of the week he alternated between uneasy sleep and a troubled, confused wakefulness. He was afraid of being kidnaped and suffering physical harm. He mumbled about making a scheduled visit to Washington, calling for the railroad schedules. He rambled on about his business plans. His condition did not seem to im-

14

prove as the days went by: on Tuesday he was seen engaged in a futile attempt to read a newspaper while holding it upside down. By that weekend the family considered the situation desperate, and he was taken to a sanitarium. He offered no resistance.

After his first decent night's sleep in a week at the sanitarium, he awoke the next morning much calmer and more rational. His condition was vastly improved. Yet it soon became clear that he had undergone a radical psychological change. Although he dressed himself as easily and as meticulously as he always had, he had no conscious memory of anything from his past, including his name. His speaking vocabulary consisted of a few basic words; his passive vocabulary was that of a very young child. He had to be told the names of everyday objects such as household items, as well as their uses. But he learned with astonishing speed, and once he learned something he did not forget it. His vocabulary of practical, concrete words burgeoned. Because one of the hospital attendants was a German immigrant, Scott pronounced many words with a German accent, but otherwise his progress was swift and solid. He learned to write a very elementary prose. He did not have to learn table manners; he conducted himself impeccably at meals, although he couldn't imagine why.

Once again his family were strangers to him. He did not recognize his fiancee, although he stoutly maintained that he knew her and that there was no one in the world he wanted more to be with. Yet he remembered nothing at all about their relationship, nor did he understand the notion of engagement or marriage. There were some people whose company he had enjoyed before his accident, and now he seemed particularly to enjoy their visits, though again he couldn't say why.

Although he proved himself to be a quick study with the concrete, he had to struggle with the abstract. Within a couple of months he was able to read newspaper accounts of everyday events with facility, but anything more complex—as in the editorials, for instance—was largely a mystery to him. In somewhat the same sense, he learned a great deal of arithmetic but very little mathematics. Before his accident he had been awkward with his hands. He had played billiards badly and had been quite incapable of drawing or carving a figure. After the accident he played billiards with admirable skill, sketched very creditably, and indulged himself happily in some highly creative woodworking. He could still play his banjo and sing songs that he had learned as a boy, yet he could not associate any of this activity with anything in his past.

Anomalies of this sort were very trying for him, but he maintained his equanimity, conducting himself with the same affability and thoughtfulness that he had shown before his accident.

His attitude toward religion reverted after the accident to the rather militant atheism that he had professed some three years before. In discussing the subject with Dr. Dana, he displayed what the doctor described as "considerable dialectic skill and logical power" despite his relative inability to handle abstract concepts. He also displayed some emotion, particularly "a special repugnance to any form of religion," which his family said had been characteristic of him in the earlier years.

The way in which he conducted ordinary, practical conversations was perfectly normal in terms of his alertness and responsiveness. But he could not avoid revealing the extraordinary gaps in his everyday knowledge. At various times, for example, it became clear that he didn't know what the sun was, or why it seemed to move; what the moon and the stars were, and why *they* seemed to move; who (and indeed *what*) other people were, and how they were related to him; what a mushroom was, and how it differed from a stone; what finger rings were, and why people wore them; where wood came from, and metal, and milk, and twine. In short, he lacked the storehouse of common knowledge that normal adults take for granted. And this made him very impatient.

But this impatience was with himself, not with others. Under the circumstances, his equanimity was a marvel to behold. He never flew into a rage, never grew inarticulate under the strain. He showed no tendency to delirium or hallucination and in general, Dr. Dana reported, "was not in the slightest degree demented." His physical health was excellent, and he slept well, evidently without dreaming. The only notable physical peculiarity was his habit, when excited, of moving his head about as if his collar were too tight—an amplified version of an old idiosyncracy.

Each week he paid Dr. Dana a visit or two, in his office. Since the doctor was wary of embarking on any therapy prematurely, their conversations were fairly desultory. As soon as his patient was able to get around town by himself, the doctor suggested that he might drop by the office where he had worked and reacquaint himself with some of his former fellow workers and with some of his former duties. Scott did so, but the experience failed to restore any of his memories.

On three occasions somewhat later, Dr. Dana resorted to hypnotism. The first effort was futile, but the second and third resulted in a shallow hypnotic sleep. While in the trance Scott was instructed to do certain things upon coming out of it—such as walking around the table, opening a door, rubbing his eyes—and to remember his past at a particular time that evening. He carried out the minor instructions to the letter, but when the appointed hour for total recall arrived in the evening, instead of remembering anything from his past, he merely stated, "Dr. Dana told me to remember something, but I can't do it."

At the suggestion of a friend, a professor of psychology, the doctor advised Scott to copy out some of his old love letters, some of the prayers he had said in his childhood, and some of the account sheets that he had prepared some years before at work. What he hoped to accomplish is obvious enough, but the exercise had no effect on Scott whatsoever.

And then, one evening just three months after the accident, the old Peter Scott came back. He and his brother were on their way home after paying a visit to his fiancee. (After they had left, she reported later, she had cried in despair over his condition, feeling that he would never recover.) In the carriage Scott complained that one side of his head felt numb yet tingling, the way a limb feels when it's "asleep." Gradually this feeling, and non-feeling, spread through his whole head. He slumped drowsily in his seat, although without falling asleep. On their arrival home he had to be carried to bed like a drunkard. He fell into a deep sleep that lasted some twelve hours. When he awoke late the next morning his memory and his old personality were fully restored, except of course that the preceding three months were a complete blank.

When he visited Dr. Dana in his office on the following day, for instance, he did not know him, since the acquaintance with the doctor was limited to the period of amnesia. That three-month gap, however, was now the only abnormal gap in his knowledge—sun, moon, stars, people, mushrooms, finger rings, wood, metal, milk and twine were all back in their accustomed places. Delighted with his recovery, Dr. Dana discharged him and, as the doctor reported later in his journal article, Scott "at once resumed his old work and habits and has continued perfectly well up to the present time."

Helene Smith, 1899

Helene Smith was, to put it mildly, an incurable romantic. Or at least part of her was. The other part was very businesslike, practical, intelligent, mature and highly competent. She held an important job with a European business firm in the 1890s, and no woman could have kept such a position and have been incompetent, at least without indestructible family connections, which Helene didn't have, or without engaging in extracurricular activities, which Helene wouldn't do.

Nonetheless, however great her competence, her work evidently provided little or no opportunity for her creative imagination. She found that kind of opportunity outside office hours with a group of spiritualists who quickly recognized her potential as a medium. Indeed, she joined several such groups and was the darling of them all. And the attention, even adulation, lavished upon her greatly enhanced her natural tendency to hallucinate.

That tendency had first come to light when she was only ten, shortly after she had been attacked by a ferocious dog. The attack had done her no physical harm, for the dog had been beaten off in the nick of time by a tall, dark and very romantic-looking stranger; but the terror of the moment lived with her long thereafter. From that time on, when she was frightened, she would seek refuge in hallucinations starring the romantic stranger, who eventually took on the name of Leopold. He proved to be not only a great comfort but also a fascinating companion, bringing to her conscious mind colorful stories which she may have known but had forgotten. After she began attending seances, Leopold's character blossomed, and her hallucinations grew ever richer in fancy embroidery. Her case became a celebrated one. At least seven books were published on it around the turn of the century, including one by a Swiss professor of psychology named Flournoy (*Des Indes à la Planète Mars*; Geneva, 1899), on which this brief account is based.

18

Early in her career as a medium Helene stayed awake during the sittings. Although her clairvoyance was quite successful—she revealed many harmless little things about people in the group and members of their families, things that they felt she simply couldn't have known about by any ordinary means—her accounts of her hallucinations were rather sketchy and generally unsatisfactory. But then Leopold took over. Instead of staying awake, she now went into deep trances about which she would remember nothing afterward. During these trances she would give detailed accounts of incidents in her other lives, of which there seemed to be three besides her own and Leopold's.

One of these was set in the fourteenth century, when, as Helene entranced described it, she was Simandini, daughter of an Arab sheik and wife of Sivrouka, ruler of the principality of Kanara, in India. Her descriptions of her luxurious living in this Xanadu were laced with phrases in Hindu and Arabic, with some of the latter written out in Arabic script. Further, the descriptions included a vast amount of meticulous detail, which was checked against historical sources and found to be substantially correct. But one of these sources, a rare and venerable history which included some Hindu and Arabic, may have been available to Helene earlier, and Leopold's power of recall undoubtedly was far better than hers.

Her role in the second "other life" was similarly radiant. She was the eighteenth century's Queen Marie Antoinette, consort to Europe's most splendid king, doyenne to its most brilliant court, and ultimately proud victim to its great leveler, the guillotine. Here again the descriptions were marvelously detailed, but in this case the detail, much more easily checked, was found to be more imaginative than accurate. The court imposter Cagliostro, for instance—with whom Leopole seemed to identify—curiously knew no Italian and was acquainted with very little of his own colorful and meretricious history. Nevertheless the descriptions, if not literally factual, were generally true to the tenor of the period and in any case were quite beyond anything that could be expected of the rather staid and inhibited Helene Smith.

For her third other life she traveled not back in time but outward in space, becoming the reincarnation of the dead son of one of her fellow spiritualists. The young man had been sent to Mars after his death and now was back with a detailed report on the flora and fauna and the civilization on that planet. Again the detail was quite abundant although, some seventy years before space probes, it hardly could be checked out. Its accuracy, however, was brought rather seriously into question by the fact that it included information on the Martians' language, which an analysis showed to be essentially European and indeed mostly French.

It seems, in short, that Leopold was the rascal that Helene could never bring herself to be. His was the fertile imagination to which she herself could never give free rein. He offered the protection she needed, the comfort she wanted, the advice she sought, the courage she lacked. Flournoy considered him quite different from Helene, "having a character more personal, an individuality more marked, and an existence more positive."

For all his manly character, however, Leopold never took over full muscular control of the body. He never fully "emerged." He was, Flournoy concluded, almost as much a part of Helene as her heart or her brain, rooted as he was in her childhood, in her fears, her desires, her fantasies. Leopold surely was only a figment of her imagination. Yet there were times—for example, during one of Leopold's brilliant monologues at a seance—when the professor felt like asking, will the real Helene Smith please stand up?

Charles Warren, 1901

A distressing aspect of some cases of multiple personality is the physical suffering involved. An observer, watching one personality writhing in pain, may be sure, frustratingly sure, that another personality can offer relief, even euphoria, just on the other side of dissociation. In some cases the emergence of another personality may have been a form of escape from suffering, and in others hypnosis has brought relief. In still others, however, whatever the reason, the suffering has gone on and on and on, with deliverance hovering just beyond the invisible barrier. Such seems to have been the predicament of Charles Warren for some seventeen years.

He was hurt in a railroad accident. It was 1884 and he was 24 years old, traveling west from Chicago to settle the affairs of his recently deceased father. (His parents had separated, amicably, when he was a child.) In reporting the case to the American Medical Association at its 1901 annual meeting (and later in the AMA *Journal* for December 14 of that year), Dr. Edward Mayer could give no details on Warren's injury. All that Warren could remember during their many interviews was a grinding crash, a feeling of being thrown across the car, and blackout. The blackout lasted seventeen years, until February, 1901. No information on the first five of those years was ever obtained, from Warren or anyone else. What Warren carried with him into the blackout consisted of his name and basic functional abilities such as eating and walking and talking, and nothing else.

For the record, therefore, his new life began in 1889, when he met his future wife in Pittsburgh, where he now lived and worked. Two years later he married her. Ultimately it devolved upon her to provide Dr. Mayer, who did not meet Warren until after February, 1901, with most of the available information on the 1889-1901 period. She had not had a very gay time of it. Her husband, despite his conscientious efforts to be a good provider and his affectionate consideration for his

21

wife and children, was not very easy to live with. His moods could be so extreme that at times she was afraid to leave the children alone with him. His usual mood was one of depression and anxiety. His persistent headaches, evidently impervious to medication, were so sharply painful as to drive him almost into a frenzy. Although he did no sleepwalking, his rest at night was fitful at best, with much tossing about and moaning. In the latter part of this period he suffered from a liver ailment that caused severe pain even between attacks, and as a result his restlessness at night grew so bad that no one could sleep in the same room with him.

In addition he seems to have been subject to frequent petit mal attacks. During a conversation he would stop talking in mid-sentence and stare into space with an intent expression and fixed eyes. After a few moments he would resume the conversation, completing the sentence that he had started. Although these brief seizures caused him no physical pain, his knowledge of them was a source of embarrassment and mental anguish. Apparently he was never free from a gnawing fear concerning his condition, especially a fear that he might have to be committed to an institution.

The seizures were not always so brief. Although he habitually left his family only to go to work (he was a teetotaler), one Sunday afternoon in 1892 he left the house unexpectedly and did not come back until Monday evening. He could offer no explanation of his absence other than a vague recollection that he had done some riding. He didn't know where he had done it, or how or why. The following year he took an even longer sabbatical. After working as a hired hand on a farm and as a laborer at a sawmill, by 1893 he had joined his brother-in-law in a housepainting business. One day, in the middle of a job, he climbed down from his ladder and disappeared, presumably headed for the nearest restroom. But when he hadn't returned by quitting time, the brother-in-law had to go home and tell his sister that poor Charlie had evidently taken to wandering again. A couple of days later a postal card arrived from a small town in eastern Pennsylvania (where he had been born). He was visiting his mother, Warren informed his wife, and would be home in another day or two. He was as good as his word, although he had some explaining to do. He had never told his wife that his mother was alive, since he hadn't known it himself.

On February 23, 1901, in the early evening, he suffered an acute attack of his liver ailment, which the family doctor had diagnosed as "hepatic abscess." In addition to the constant pain, the faintest touch anywhere near the liver was excruciating. As he was pacing the dining-room floor, his daughter happened to knock a lamp off a table and he made a desperate effort to catch it before it hit the floor. As he started toward it he suddenly cried out, "Oh, my head!" and fell down in a faint. The family put him to bed and called the doctor, who came at once but could not revive him. His pulse and respiration were normal, however, and at about four in the morning he awoke briefly and then fell into a deep sleep. The doctor, reassured, returned home.

When Warren awoke again later that morning he asked his wife whether he was seriously hurt. She replied with a puzzled no. He asked what hospital this was, and whether she was the nurse assigned to him. To her reply that he was at home and that she was his wife he responded rather irritably that he was in no mood for joking. He asked her to call for the doctor. After she had asked one of the children to fetch the doctor, she returned to the room and asked him if he would like to see any of their four children. Seeing that, unaccountably, she wasn't joking, he protested that he was not married and that it wasn't very nice to tell an injured bachelor of 24 that he had fathered four children. Protesting in her turn, his wife produced a mirror, their marriage license, and some photographs taken of him at various times over the past twelve years with members of the family. The doctor then arrived, with the children hard on his heels. Warren recognized neither the doctor nor any of the children. But their impassioned testimony eventually convinced him that a great deal of mysterious water must have flowed under the bridge since his accident.

For the doctor perhaps the greatest surprise was the fact that his patient was no longer in any pain. All signs of the hepatic abscess had completely disappeared. Where before the merest rouch had been excruciating, he could now punch Warren in the abdomen without causing any serious discomfort. Reluctant to handle a case like this alone, the next day he referred Warren to Dr. Mayer, who in turn called in members of the Pittsburgh Academy of Medicine.

A physical examination resulted in a thoroughly clean bill of health. Questions about Warren's childhood, which he now remembered in great detail, turned up nothing remarkable. His current situation was quite difficult for him, since he failed to recognize old friends, could not find his way about the neighborhood (much less the city), and on one embarrassing occasion had trouble gaining entrance to a house because he couldn't find a knocker on the front door and didn't know about electric bells. In the grocery store that he and his wife had started a couple of years before because of his illness, he had to relearn the inventory, the names of customers, the various prices, and so on. Once he did, however, he took over management of the store and even was able to improve on his wife's bookkeeping.

Since the store clearly would not provide enough money, he got a job but, having lost all the skills that he had acquired in his other state, he was limited to paltry wages. He very quickly grew discouraged and began having depressing dreams that revolved about the possibility of his being committed, the weird unreality of his life, the puzzling remarks of his friends, and the unpleasant newspaper publicity visited upon him and his family. He held up under the pressure for just two weeks. On March 8 he failed to come home from work until nine in the evening, when he staggered into the house in a state of exhaustion. At five that afternoon, he said, he had suddenly discovered that he was in Greensburg, some thirty miles southeast of Pittsburgh, and had caught the next train home. He had no recollection of anything he might have done in Greensburg, nor could he offer any explanation of his going there. (Weeks later it was discovered that he had visited a wholesale grocery firm and ordered some supplies for the store. The salesman who had taken the order testified that he seemed in a daze at the time.) The next morning, March 9, his wife gave him $25 to buy some groceries for the store.

Dr. Mayer's report ends at this point on a discouraging note: "He left home and did not return. No trace or word from him has since reached us, and he seems to have entirely disappeared from the face of the earth." But there is also a laconic, cryptic footnote, which looks as though it must have been added hastily just before publication: "Later. —September 2, 1901, Mr. W. came back to Pittsburgh."

George Robertson, 1902

Whatever else may be said of George Robertson's several personalities, they seem to have been among the most restless on record. Details of the case are difficult to organize largely because he/they spent so much time hopping about the country. Indeed, many of the changes from one personality to another took place on trains.

On April 2, 1902, Dr. J.A. Gilbert and his colleague Dr. Cobb accepted on referral a 22-year-old male patient suffering from a severe blow on the head. The town was Portland, Oregon, and in February George Robertson, employed by a nearby lumber mill, had fallen from a barge and struck his head on a floating log. This led to his hospitalization and referral to Drs. Gilbert and Cobb, as well as to Dr. Gilbert's report of the case, later in 1902, in the New York *Medical Record*.

It was now some five weeks after the accident, and George had been in and out of the hospital three times. He was still having sharp, persistent headaches, and his memory was playing tricks on him. He recalled hitting his head, being stunned for a moment, recovering and crawling onto the log, being helped ashore, and catching a streetcar to take him to the hospital (sturdy types, these loggers). What he did not recall was the three weeks from that moment until his third and last departure from the hospital—including his being taken from the streetcar and making the rest of the trip to the hospital in an ambulance, his waking up the next morning and deliriously chasing rats in his bed (he had no liquor or drug problems), his sudden recovery and release, his two readmissions. Another thing he didn't remember was picking up his wages from the lumber company; but he had a copy of the signed receipt in his pocket.

The doctors suggested that hypnosis might help to restore his memory. Whatever his misgivings, George was frustrated enough to agree, although his residual resistance was sufficiently strong to keep Dr. Gilbert busy for half an hour before the stubborn logger finally went

25

under. During the trance he was able to answer detailed questions about the missing three weeks. Encouraged, the doctor ended the trance by instructing him to wake up gradually and to feel well in every respect.

Instead he awoke very abruptly, giving every indication of startled fear and confusion. He didn't recognize the doctors or his surroundings, nor could he understand how he could have gotten into this predicament. The doctors, once they had recovered from their own surprise, began questioning him. He was under the impression, they discovered, that this was a Saturday in September, 1899, and that only "yesterday" he had been in Glenrock, Wyoming, quarreling with his father. He knew nothing at all about the time in between.

During the following six or seven weeks he was kept under observation, by no means against his will. The doctors engaged him in long and frequent periods of intense questioning, often using hypnosis to bridge the many memory gaps. Although the information that they extracted was fragmentary and disordered, they were resolved to do what they could to line up the bits and pieces into a continuous history, since they felt that this would be an essential preliminary step in any therapy. Eventually they did arrive at a reasonably coherent chronology of George's past, which involved at least three personalities, each unaware of the others. George 1 was mentally alert, robust and jolly, fully knowledgeable about his relatives and the events of his youth, and eager to get enough education to raise him from his current status of common laborer. George 2 was neurasthenic, subject to spells of deep lethargy and to constant headache, quiet and retiring, pious and rather melancholy, yet ambitious to capitalize (also through education) on his natural mechanical aptitude and inventiveness; he knew very little about his relatives, and what little he did know was limited to periods after his middle teens. George 3 seemed to be chronically ill, plagued by insatiable hunger and sharp pains in his head and abdomen; thoroughly lacking any sense of ambition, he was a hobo, taking odd jobs only when his choice was between work and starvation, and his reply to those who asked where he came from was that he "didn't come from anyplace." (One of the features of this case, incidentally, was that all of the personalities answered to the same name.) There may have been a George 4, but of this the doctors could never be sure. In this fourth, semidelirious state he was in such pain and suffered from such burning thirst that he could never give them any information. Fortunately these periods were brief and infrequent, but for that very reason, among others, the doctors could not determine the relationship of this state to the other three, if indeed it was a separate state.

The history, as pieced together by the doctors, began in Nemeha City, Nebraska, where George 1 was born in December, 1879. His mother died when he was three, and his father later remarried. At the time of his hospitalization his living relatives were his father and stepmother, a brother, a half-sister, a stepsister, and all four grandparents. They seem to have been about as loosely knit a group as you're likely to find this side of the alligator. The remarriage may have caused some problems: George 1 had trouble with his father, and at fourteen he ran away to his mother's relatives, who lived in another small Nebraska town, Crawford. After a couple of years in Crawford he may have felt depressed about overstaying his welcome, for one day in the railroad depot George 2 emerged and took a train out of town. It was April, 1896.

This was the start of his active wanderlust. His first stop was Edgemont, South Dakota. After spending a few weeks there, he went on to New Castle, Wyoming. New Castle apparently proved no more spellbinding than Edgemont. Within another few weeks he was on a train bound for Cambria, Wyoming. What untold delights Cambria might have offered, George 2 never found out. On the train George 1 emerged. Alarmed at finding himself on a train that he couldn't remember boarding, he got off at Cambria only long enough to catch the next train to Crawford. His welcome there, however, may have been less than heartwarming, for he soon took to the rails again, traveling from town to town in southern Nebraska and northern Kansas. In May, 1898, he was in Lincoln, Nebraska, where he enlisted for service in the latest male fad, the recently declared Spanish-American War. From there the U.S. Army sent him, presumably for training, to Chickamauga, Georgia, but he was to prove a rather unreliable recruit.

One day in early June he fell asleep under a tree and awoke as George 3. He immediately started traveling, without the formality of a farewell address to the Army, through a succession of towns in Tennessee, Kentucky, Illinois, Indiana and Missouri. On a train headed for Kansas City George 1 emerged, once again finding himself on a train that he couldn't remember boarding. He may have panicked and jumped off the train before it arrived in Kansas City proper. At any rate, not long thereafter George 3 returned to find himself on the bluffs overlooking Kansas City. After a brief search for the nearest railroad tracks, he caught a freight, crossed the Kansas River—and changed back to George 1.

George 1, being the one with the homing instinct, immediately headed for relatives in Havensville, Kansas, only to discover on his ar-

rival that they wanted no truck with him. Thus rejected, he went on to
Liberty, Nebraska, where he got a job and settled down for several
weeks. And then one day George 3 emerged, found to his delight that
there was money in his pocket, and naturally used some of it to buy a
train ticket, this time to Red Cloud, Nebraska. On the train he was replaced by another personality, probably George 2, who later remembered being in Red Cloud, although he could recall no details; as a result, this period is essentially a blank.

George 3 re-emerged in the autumn of 1898 in a field of oats not
far from Oxford, Nebraska. During the next eleven or twelve months
the three personalities must have alternated rather rapidly, for later all
three had some disjointed memories of the period and none had anything approaching a continuous recollection. They continued to move
about, from Oxford to Mascot to Holdredge, where George 1 emerged
fully and, of course, immediately headed for home. Home this time
was Glenrock, Wyoming, where his father was now living. He apparently stayed there only briefly. During a quarrel between his father and
stepmother, he joined in, and his father struck him a heavy blow on the
head. George 2 emerged and immediately headed for the railroad station. George 1 was not to reappear until that fateful day in Portland in
April 1902.

George 2 traveled about Nebraska, South Dakota and Wyoming for
the next eight or nine months. In Cheyenne, In June, 1900, he was replaced by George 3, who took a train to Denver, where he was replaced
by George 2, who took a train to San Francisco, from which he took
another train to Oakland on which he was replaced by George 3, who
took a train to Portland, where he was replaced by George 2, who got a
job as a logger and, in February, 1902, fell from a barge and struck his
head on a floating log. If this brief account of those thirty months
leaves the reader a bit dizzy, one can imagine how George must have
felt after living through them. *Any* George.

One event in this period was George 2's reenlistment in the Army,
in San Francisco (the first enlistment, in Lincoln, was as George 1).
After the reenlistment he had been replaced by George 3 long enough
to make him forget the Army and to start him on the road to Portland.
In May, 1902, Dr. Gilbert wrote dozens of letters requesting information that could confirm the biographical data that he had obtained
from the three Georges, including a letter to the Army post at San
Francisco. In response the Army picked up George, who by now
seemed pretty well integrated, and took him to Vancouver, Washington,

to be tried for desertion. The doctor followed him there and finally obtained a promise of his release on medical grounds after what must have been some very difficult conversations. When George was brought to him, he was surprised to discover that it was George 2, but he was able, through hypnosis, to patch all three together again.

At the time the doctor's report was published, George was still being held in a military jail, impatiently awaiting the conclusion of what the doctor considered mere bureaucratic formalities. Presumably he was released before long, probably into the doctor's custody. Whether he was ever cured is not recorded, but at least he now had someone who was willing, even eager, to look after him.

John Kinsel, 1903

For most of us there are only two mutually exclusive states: we're either asleep or awake. There are intermediate stages between the two, of course, but these ordinarily are transitional, as when someone sleepily but doggedly thrusts a right foot into a left slipper while getting out of bed in the early morning. But for John Kinsel there was a third state. Here was a man who, when asked by his doctor in the middle of the morning, "Well, John, how are you this morning?" could and did reply, "I'm asleep; I've been asleep since eight o'clock." Or, on another occasion, "I woke up asleep this morning."

The doctor was a psychologist named George Cutten, who reported the case at great length in *The Psychological Review* for September, 1903, after much painstaking research into John's background and with unstinting cooperation from John's friends and relatives, as well as from John himself.

John was born on a farm in New England in 1873. His robust father had worked hard, had prospered—and had drunk eight to ten glasses of homemade hard cider every day of his adult life without (so far as anyone knew) ever being drunk. This kind of relentless drinking was a family tradition, which also included frequent resort to brandy, but there were only two full-time drunkards in the family. John was not one of them, in the sense that he never became a long-term habitual drunkard, yet he did not completely share the family immunity. This oversight caused him some difficulties in his early twenties, including the loss of his fiancee.

Both his father and his mother, who was generally unwell and mildly neurotic, had family histories riddled with instances of emotional and mental instability, drunkenness, epilepsy and paralysis, as well as a case of cataracts. If there is anything to heredity, it may have been especially fortunate that John was an only child. Although his normally good health was interrupted at the age of four by an almost fatal attack of dysentery and, not long thereafter, by an accident involving a head injury, Dr. Cutten did not consider these experiences important in John's psychomedical history: "We might find a traumatic origin for his epileptiform condition here if it were necessary, but his family history would make this superfluous; for not only are we able to charge it to heredity, but given such a heredity we would look for it in his life."

Nevertheless, the age of four seems to have marked a turning point in the record of John's physical and emotional well-being. A congenital nervous condition became much aggravated, and he developed a very bad stutter that plagued him constantly for the next eight years and then intermittently for the rest of his life (or at least until 1903, the date of the report, at which time it was still a minor nuisance at best). He also developed a habit of vivid dreaming and precarious sleepwalking; one night, in his tenth year, he and his worried dog walked half a mile over very rough terrain before he woke up at two in the morning and returned home, presumably to the dog's great relief. He had an inordinate thirst, downing water at the rate of three to five quarts a day, and consequently suffered from polyuria. He had continual headaches, especially during high school, which often were terribly painful and could be relieved only by vomiting. In college, where the headaches (at least the physical headaches) were less severe, he suffered from persistent nosebleeds. Many of his health problems doubtless stemmed from his defective vision, which was never better than a third of normal until he underwent treatment for cataracts in 1899. One apparent result of this condition was the peculiar characteristic suggested in the opening paragraph: for a long time, until his senior year in college (1896), the eyes of his secondary personality were always closed. For this reason he and the doctor, as well as his friends and relatives, referred to his secondary state as being "asleep," even during and after his senior year, when the secondary personality kept his eyes open. And thus it was that he could tell the doctor, "I woke up asleep this morning," and have the remark accepted as sensible. For our purposes here, it will probably be easiest to distinguish the two personalities, when the distinction is important, by adopting this language and calling the primary personality "John Awake" and the secondary personality "John Asleep."

Dr. Cutten never arrived at a completely satisfactory explanation of John Asleep's ability to "see" with his eyes closed. Most of his achievements, such as wandering about on campus without stumbling or bumping into things, could be explained by the presumption that his eyes weren't fully closed and by his extraordinarily acute hearing. But

there was a residue of incidents, such as seeing (or visually comprehend-
ing?) something above his eye level, which the baffled doctor had to
assign to the category of unsolved mysteries.

John Asleep had the advantage of John Awake, for he was the
"continuous" personality, conscious of what was going on regardless of
who was on deck, and thus able to remember events in continuity.
John Awake, in contrast, knew about only the things that had occurred
when he was in control. He was particularly at a disadvantage in college
during examinations for which John Asleep had done the cramming.
On one occasion he "awoke" an hour or so before a particularly important exam, and it was only by getting the doctor to hypnotize him that
he was able to pass it as John Asleep.

This subordination of John Awake was unfortunate because the
characters of the two personalities were quite different, his being by far
the more agreeable. He was quiet, good-humored, considerate of others,
and in general readily distinguishable from John Asleep, an incorrigible
boor who usually made a point of spreading discomfort at every opportunity among those whom he listed as his enemies, in a list that included
everyone at one time or another. Yet when he was in a halfway decent
humor John Asleep was better company, for he was brighter than John
Awake, wittier, and much less inhibited. At times he could even be
quite clownish, to the vast amusement of his fellow students, who were
more or less acquainted with John's dichotomous condition and who
sometimes took good-natured advantage of it.

Formal education was a heavy burden for John, whose minimal
eyesight turned reading and writing into exhausting chores. Yet it was
unavoidable if he was to enter the ministry, which at the time was his
most accessible escape route from a life of farming. He consistently displayed a great distaste for farming, although his vacations on the farm
invariably saw a great improvement in his condition. His father's pros-
perity had proved sufficient to put him through high school and to pay
most of his way through college. What his father could not do was to
help him with his studies, and for this he relied on a roommate who
played Horatio to his Hamlet with almost unbelievable understanding,
tolerance and self-sacrificing devotion.

A peculiarity of this case is the time that it took for the secondary
personality to develop. In most cases the other personality appears
suddenly, unexpectedly, with a set of characteristics about as complete
as he or she will ever have. But in John's case the process took something over two years, passing through four fairly distinct stages. During

his sophomore year he spent his secondary-state periods lying down, with his eyes closed; he could be quite talkative and animated, but he always looked as though he were asleep. During most of his junior year his secondary states were similar except that he sat up ordinarily, instead of lying down. In part of his junior and senior years he took to walking about, though still with his eyes closed. It was not until about Christmas in his senior year that John Asleep fully emerged and, for about the next year and a half, conducted his portion of John's everyday business quite creditably, with eyes open and with unrestricted mobility. During this period the two Johns shared the time on deck about equally.

Another peculiarity of the case was John Asleep's virtuosity in improvising doggerel, somewhat resembling the talent of idiot savants for arithmetical calculation. When the spell was on him, he could produce riming, scanning verse just as fast as he could talk. One Sunday afternoon in April, 1895, for instance, he and four other students ran into foul weather during a sail and had to spend the night in an open boat anchored offshore. The next morning, on their way home, John fell "asleep" in the bow and began spouting doggerel like a runaway recording. The students were in no mood or condition to faithfully transcribe their Homer manqué for posterity, but they did manage to catch a few small samples, one of which is given here to suggest the flavor of his outpourings. It may not quite rank with Robert Browning, but it compares favorably with Edgar Guest, especially when one considers its genesis. There's even a touch of Coleridge about it:

> Herbert Alger had a scheme,
> a wild, fantastic, fevered dream.
> He thought if westward he should sail,
> before a strong, propitious gale,
> that he would find a wondrous land,
> where gold lay sparkling in the sand;
> green banknotes grew on all the trees
> and rustled there in every breeze.

John Awake had no such talent, of course, and he knew about John Asleep's performance only by report, since he had no direct knowledge of anything that his gifted double said or did.

He did a lot of sleepwalking in the latter part of his sophomore year, then almost none at all during his summer vacation on the farm, and then a lot again during his junior year. At first his midnight and small-hours visits to other dormitories were considered amusing, but before long he got to be a nuisance and for his own protection his long-suffering roommate took to locking the door at night and keeping the key on his person. John fell in with the plan readily, and from then on his extracellular sleepwalking depended on his roommate's occasional forgetfulness.

Meanwhile it was getting harder to "wake" him. Until now his fellow students had been able to do so by gently rubbing his face, but this was becoming less and less effective. As the rubbing grew less gentle with successive failures in bringing him to, and then was augmented by slapping, his resistance seemed to increase until finally his friends resorted to hitting him in the buttocks with large books, in slapstick style. John Awake was not at all offended by these therapeutic spankings, since he welcomed anything that would shorten the blackouts that so distressed him, and for a while the technique worked splendidly. Then it too began to diminish in effectiveness and was finally abandoned after one of his friends spent an entire afternoon spanking him at intervals with a formidable Latin dictionary but without bringing him out of his trance. After this he was left to his own devices.

During this year John exhibited a new, remarkable and peculiar talent for memorizing. After merely reading a passage in Greek prose, such as that of Herodotus, John Awake could fall asleep and, after emerging as John Asleep, quote it in full and with perfect accuracy. But the really *peculiar* peculiarity about this talent was that he sometimes would continue beyond the passage, not quoting from the text any longer but instead improvising a flow of nonsense Greek made up of words chosen at random from John Awake's limited Greek vocabulary.

In the latter part of his junior year, in the spring of 1896, John Awake (but never John Asleep) suffered perhaps a dozen serious attacks of epilepsy, some violent enough to throw him down, others deep enough to render him unconscious. In addition to these grand mal seizures, he was bothered by an undetermined number of petit mal attacks. During the summer vacation on the farm, however, this aspect of his illness essentially disappeared, and he returned to the campus in the fall apparently able and clearly willing to complete his final year.

It was in December that John Asleep finally emerged in full flower. One morning John Awake left his roommate in their dormitory room, promising to be back very shortly. He was gone for several hours, however, and returned in what his roommate considered a very puzzling condition. This John was in a boisterous mood and slightly drunk, whereas John Awake was always rather withdrawn and scrupulously sober. Yet his eyes were not closed, and he bustled about with perfectly normal competence. John Asleep, the roommate decided, had finally managed to get his eyes open.

A cousin of his was in town, John said, and he had come back to the room for just a moment before going out again to pay the cousin a visit. His roommate, worried over how he might behave in his present condition, remonstrated. When his objections were ignored, he placed himself against the door to prevent John's leaving. This greatly angered John Asleep, who cajoled, then threatened, and finally, after picking up a large, empty water bottle, advanced on his roommate with bottle upraised and with mayhem written all over his face. When the intrepid roommate stood his ground, however, John subsided and concluded meekly that he didn't want to visit his cousin after all.

This incident was to prove fairly typical. With his new vision (still poor, but better than with his eyes closed) John Asleep found many more opportunities to be flamboyantly contentious. Some days later he got into a violent quarrel with a classmate whose own fuse was quite short, especially where John Asleep was concerned. When John's roommate interceded, John took down a sword from the Revolutionary War, kept in the room as a wall decoration, and began jabbing it at him with alarming vigor and skill and yet with what seemed a deliberate effort to avoid actually hitting him. When the roommate grappled with him and they fell to the floor with John on the bottom, John lost heart, went limp, and asked in a childish whine what had happened to his cigar, which had disappeared in the melee. The original object of his wrath, the classmate, stole away as inconspicuously as possible. As for John Awake, he would know of such incidents only by the way that he sometimes felt on emergence (angry, excited, perhaps disheartened) and of course by being told of them. He winced a lot.

John Awake might change places with John Asleep any time and anywhere, although dissociation was more likely during periods of stress, excitement, or exhaustion. The dissociations could be very frequent and brief, occurring several times in as many minutes and each lasting only a few tens of seconds. They also could be quite lengthy, as in the week when John Asleep emerged early Wednesday morning, went about his business as usual, attended his classes and a symphony concert, and eventually turned the body over to John Awake late Sunday morning, in the middle of a sermon (when he may have especially wanted to surrender the ears).

With all this experience, John Asleep grew into quite a man of the world during the senior year. His character evidently softened a good deal, and during the second semester his friends found it increasingly difficult to know with full confidence just who was on deck at any given time. Before long the roommate and Dr. Cutten began experiencing the same difficulty, and soon thereafter even John himself wasn't always sure, at least until he had introspectively checked his memory: if there were gaps in it, he knew that he must be John Awake.

During these last college months John evidently was an object of great interest to the medical profession, being examined by a variety of experts ranging from oculists to psychologists. On the basic cause of his problems there were, of course, about as many opinions as there were experts. The oculists, however, generally agreed that his eye trouble was not the cause, at least in any organic way. A neurologist opted for epilepsy but apparently failed to assign any specific cause for the epilepsy. The most interesting speculation was offered by a physician who suggested that John's problem was unintentional self-hypnosis. When John looked at anything, this doctor pointed out, he thrust his head down and looked upward, in a kind of glower, because of the location of the cataracts. This position of the head disposes many people to hypnosis, so much so that it was a standard attitude for subjects to take before entrancement by hypnotists of a then popular school. Dr. Cutten found this idea fascinating, but he cast his vote for epilepsy.

Near the end of his senior year John became engaged to a very proper girl without telling her about his personality problems. By this time the two personalities were sufficiently similar, and he had become sufficiently adroit in covering up such differences as might be noticeable, for him to get away with the concealment. Since she lived some seventy miles from the college, she saw little of his friends; when she did see them, they were cooperatively circumspect. But he had some close calls. On one occasion John Awake, while visiting her for two or three days, took her little brother to the woods on a rabbit-trapping expedition. It was John Asleep who returned to the house, where—since he was still the less inhibited of the two personalities—he tried to embrace her in the presence of her family. She resisted with a coy gaiety that barely concealed her embarrassment. Later, back at the college, John Awake couldn't understand it when her weekly letter failed to arrive. Suspecting that his unpredictable double may have put his foot in it during the blackout, he asked his roommate to question John Asleep, when he next emerged, about his behavior on that visit. The roommate found John Asleep to be a mine of relevant information, of course, and with a flurry of apologies John Awake managed gradually to restore his intended's equanimity.

But not for very long. That summer he took on some work that required some traveling. On this particular occasion John Asleep emerged in one of the small towns on the itinerary, headed for the nearest bar, got himself thoroughly sauced, and then took it into his head to hop a train and pay his sweetheart a visit. Needless to say, she was mightily offended, especially since she felt that he had deceived her into thinking that he didn't drink, what with his ecclesiastical ambitions and all. This time the subsequent flurry of apologies fell on adamantly deaf ears.

In the latter part of his senior year a graduate student in psychology offered to help him by hypnotizing him out of his trances whenever they occurred. Desperately eager to live a life more nearly approaching the normal, John hesitantly agreed. This program had its ups and downs but was hardly an enduring success: toward the end of the semester a disillusioned John Asleep was calling the graduate student "that little pimp" and was even getting testy with the solicitous Dr. Cutten. And it was after this treatment, of course, that he lost his fiancee.

In the fall of 1897, having received his college degree, John enrolled at a divinity school but, on the advice of the family physician, left in the middle of the first semester. And so, in a final bit of irony, he never did enter the ministry. Yet neither did he have to stay on the farm. Between 1899 and 1902 he underwent extensive eye treatments, including surgery, which considerably improved his vision. Perhaps because his life was less hectic now, his dissociations grew less and less frequent until, some time in 1898, they essentially ceased altogether. In the fall of 1900 he fell victim to alcoholism (or dipsomania, to use Dr. Cutten's word) but, after six months of treatment by the doctor, in which hypnosis was employed to implant a strong repugnance to alcohol in his unconscious, he recovered completely. By September, 1903, when the Cutten report was published, he was teaching in a preparatory school and apparently living (at least by contrast) a serenely happy life. Dr. Cutten's report ends with a heartening comment: "He is also said to be a successful teacher."

Victor Laval, 1904

The cause of Victor Laval's amnesia and dissociations is not clear, but plainly he spent his childhood in France during the late 1860s and early '70s, in less than ideal circumstances. His mother was unmarried, didn't know who his father was, and was "addicted to an open life of debauchery." Her maternal instincts seem to have been approximately those of a salamander. As soon as the boy could walk he spent his time roaming about the streets and begging. By the time he was fourteen he was a thief, convicted and confined in a reformatory at Saint-Urbain.

His story, reported by a French psychologist named Ribot, is cited at length by Boris Sidis in his *Multiple Personality* (Appleton, 1905). Ribot obtained his information from the records and the personnel at the half-dozen institutions in which Victor evidently spent most of his adult life. As a result the report suffers from annoying gaps and some imprecision on dates and places, but its testimony in general is quite solid and detailed.

At the reformatory Victor was assigned to work in the vineyard. One day, to keep his balance while on his knees, he placed a hand on a pile of twigs under which a snake was hiding. The startled snake slithered away, leaving behind a boy frightened out of his wits. In great agitation he ran back to the reformatory headquarters, where he fainted dead away. This turned out to be only the first in a series of attacks during which his legs grew progressively weaker until finally they became paralyzed. In this paraplegic condition he was transferred to an asylum at Bonneval.

At the reformatory he apparently had displayed his share of the sullen recalcitrance common in such environments. At the asylum he was amiable, appreciative, humbly contrite over his life of crime, and ostensibly resolved to mend his ways. In the hope that this new attitude was honest, the authorities decided that he should learn to write (he already could read passably) and should be trained in work that he could perform despite his paraplegia. During the next two months, besides working on his handwriting, he was taken to the tailor shop each morning, where he learned to sew quite skillfully. He was very diligent and conscientious, and the attendants were all pleased with his performance and behavior.

But then one morning he had an epileptic seizure that lasted, in varying degrees of severity, for two solid days. At the end of the second day he fell into a deep sleep. When he awoke the paraplegia was gone. After asking for his clothes, he dressed himself (though rather awkwardly) and tottered out of the room and down the hall. Although weak and suffering from muscular atrophy, he obviously had recovered from his paralysis. When he asked to join his buddies at work in the vineyard, some hurried questions soon revealed that he thought he was still at the reformatory and that he had been frightened by the snake just "the other day." He didn't know where he was now, nor did he recognize any of the attendants. He knew nothing of the time that had passed since his fright in the vineyard; indeed, he was quite unaware that any time *had* passed.

The attendants, knowing that hysterical people are often given to dissembling, tried to trick him into contradictions, but his story stood up under the test. They took him to the tailor shop, where he seemed thoroughly confused and totally unable to sew a stitch. When they showed him some clothes that he had worked on, he smirked and told them, in effect, to stop putting him on. This sort of thing went on for a month, until finally they were forced to accept his amnesia as genuine and he was forced to accept their account of the two missing months as true.

His personality at this time, they later testified, was much different from that which he had exhibited during those two months. Now he was uncivil, contentious, irascible and overbearing. He was also gluttonous: he had disliked wine in his earlier state, for instance, and usually had given his share to his fellow inmates, but now he drank all that he could get his hands on, his own and some of theirs as well. When he was warned that in stealing the wine he was up to his old tricks, he replied that if he was guilty of stealing, he had paid for it by going to prison.

He soon escaped, after appropriating sixty francs from the till and most of the belongings of one of the attendants. He was arrested at a railroad station about five miles outside Bonneval, just as he was about to catch a train for Paris. He did not come quietly: he was brought back to the asylum only after a good deal of scuffling and biting, and his furious antics on his return became so uncontrollable that he had to be put in solitary confinement. Eventually he wound up at another institution at Bicetre, from which he escaped, this time successfully. Turning up later in Rochefort, he enlisted in the Marine Corps, was convicted of stealing and, after a spectacular epileptic attack, was incarcerated in a military hospital. The vagaries of his personality soon attracted attention, and he was put under intensive observation. The report resulting from this period of observation identified six "states" and described his personality and behavior in each.

In the first state Victor was paralyzed, and largely without feeling, on his right side. He was garrulous, given to physical violence, and contemptuously imperious in his relations with others. He addressed everyone with the familiar *tu*, usually adding an offensive surname. He smoked constantly, seemed always to be out of tobacco, and became a great nuisance with his continual demands on others who might have some. In speech his grammar was good but his diction was atrocious, so that much of what he said was unintelligible. He could read but, because of the paralysis, could not write. He was extremely knowledgeable about current events, held drastically radical political views, was opposed to all religion, and sharply resented all displays of authority. His memory for recent details was splendid, but he could recall nothing earlier than his stay at Bicetre, except for a brief period at Bonneval just before his escape. Everything else in his history was lost in amnesia.

In his second state he was paralyzed, also with a loss of feeling, but on his left side. He labored under the delusion that it was more than a year earlier, January, 1884, and that he was back at Bicetre. He was quiet, almost withdrawn, and very respectful in dealing with others, avoiding the use of *tu* and addressing each attendant as "Monsieur." He smoked, but very moderately and unobtrusively. On political and religious questions he expressed no opinion, apparently out of embarrassment over his ignorance. He spoke well and clearly, could read normally, and wrote quite legibly. He knew nothing of Rochefort or the Marine Corps. He recalled a brief period after his arrival at Bicetre, but nothing more.

In his third state the paralysis and hemianesthia were limited to the limbs on the left side. He had receded to August, 1882, and thought himself back in an asylum at Saint-Georges de Bourg. His personality, behavior and attitudes were generally like those of his second state. His memory was restricted to a short period of intermittent illness during his twentieth year.

In his fourth state he was back in the Bonneval asylum, again paralyzed below the waist and again a tailor's apprentice. He conducted himself with a kind of sad dignity, mixed with timidity in dealing with the authorities. His diction was good but his grammar was childishly primitive. He could neither read nor write. His memory reached back to his last days at the reformatory but stopped just this side of his experience with the snake. His earlier life was a complete blank.

In his fifth state he was back in the reformatory at Saint-Urbain in 1877, fourteen years old and free of paralysis. He could read and write, and his general behavior matched the descriptions obtained from the reformatory attendants by the Rochefort investigators. He recalled his entire childhood, including his arrest and conviction, up to the encounter with the snake, the recollection of which brought on a terrifying attack of epilepsy.

From this seizure he emerged into his sixth state, which brought him close to his present stay in the institution at Rochefort. To him it was March, 1885, and he was a 22-year-old recruit in the Marine Corps. He behaved himself quite properly, being neither timid nor imperious, nor at all contentious. He spoke well and could read and write. He could recall his entire life except for the two months as a paraplegic and tailor's assistant. He did not know how to sew.

The observers and experimenters at Rochefort used hypnosis—which they called "suggestion in provoked somnambulism"—as a therapeutic tool. At this point in Victor's treatment they seemed to be having some success, although at best the process promised to be glacial. But the record ends here and, unfortunately for our curiosity, Victor Laval abruptly disappears into one of the dark recesses of history.

Thomas Hanna, 1905

Thomas Hanna was a young clergyman who lived on his family's farm in an eastern state near the turn of the century. He was quite healthy, intelligent, scholarly, and dedicated to his clerical duties. He could hardly have been more normal—until his accident. The case is reported in Boris Sidis' *Multiple Personality* (Appleton, 1905).

One Thursday evening in April, 1897, he and his brother were riding home from a nearby town in the family carriage. Noticing that something seemed to be wrong with the harness, Thomas reined in the horse and stopped the carriage to adjust the straps. As he got out of his seat his foot became entangled in a blanket on the floor, and he fell to the ground on his head, which apparently struck a rock. By the time his brother had leaped to the ground and examined him he was already quite unconscious. His breathing was so faint that his brother feared he might be dead or dying.

This indeed was the fear of the three doctors who examined him shortly after he had been carried into the bedroom of a nearby farmhouse belonging to a friend of the Hanna family. They found that his head injury was very severe and administered large doses of strychnine in an effort to revive him. At first it seemed that this radical therapy would fail, but eventually Thomas began to react. He opened his eyes, glanced about him, moved an arm, sat up in the bed, reached out toward one of the doctors and apparently tried to push him. Assuming that their patient was delirious, the doctors grabbed him and tried to force him back onto the bed. Thomas pushed back with astonishing strength—a strength much greater than might be expected even of a strong man his size in perfect health. In the ensuing melee they were unable to control him until, with the help of an experienced attendant, they were finally able to overpower him and to tie him securely onto the bed.

The doctors were astonished by more than his unaccountable strength. There was something very strange about his behavior. They would hardly have expected him to behave normally under the circumstances, but neither did he behave quite like delirious patients with whom they had had experience. For all his Herculean strength, his movements seemed uncoordinated. During the struggle he had not uttered a word, and after it he lay on the bed quietly, instead of flailing about in an attempt to free himself. As he lay there, he looked around with what seemed like curiosity. When spoken to, he showed every sign of being totally uncomprehending. On the whole, he seemed to be conducting himself not so much as a delirious patient as a newborn infant. But that, of course, was impossible.

It turned out to be not so impossible, after all. For it was Thomas Hanna who had fallen from the carriage and another personality, whom we'll call Tom, who had awakened in the farmhouse bedroom. A rather peculiar aspect of this case is that Thomas, some six months after his recovery, remembered much of this experience and his (Tom's) reactions to it throughout, and he provided the doctors with a detailed report written from his viewpoint. This report, verified by the journal notes and recollections of the doctors and of friends and relatives, forms the core of the case history.

Tom's first experience after awakening was simply one of consciousness. During these first brief moments—which, Thomas later reported, seemed like centuries—his eyes were closed, he heard no sound, he made no movement. Yet somehow he was "aware," perhaps merely of existence. He felt a kind of mental tension which, at the least, was clearly different from nonexistence.

His first sensation was that of breathing. As soon as he became aware of the process, he also recognized that he could focus his attention on it and even consciously control it. So he experimented, varying it eagerly from deep breathing to rapid gasping (and thus giving the attending doctors cause for both reassurance and alarm). At about the same time he discovered that he could hear the breathing, especially when he indulged in a kind of snorting. The anxious onlookers found this activity very unnerving, but there was nothing, they felt, that they could safely do about it.

It didn't last long, however, for Tom now became conscious of hearing things other than his breathing, and he quieted down so that he could investigate this new wonder. This in turn lasted only a moment before his eyes opened, and all sound immediately faded into the background. His overriding impression was that of color, or rather of a profusion of colors in a variety of shapes. The shapes were unrecognizable,

since only experience permits identification and Tom was not equipped
with any visual experience on which to rely. Further, nothing had any
detectable thickness, nor did Tom have any perception of distance. Indeed, he had no idea that his impressions represented anything outside
himself.

At the lower edge of his vision something moved: his own chest, as
he inhaled. In an instinctive effort to get a better look, he moved his
head. Impressed by this new sensation and the accompanying feeling
of control, he turned his head up and down and sideways ever more
vigorously until his shoulders joined in the motion and then his arms
and his fingers and finally his whole body. There was now considerable
commotion in the bed as he thrashed about exuberantly, testing his
new powers with great delight.

Concerned by all this activity, one of the doctors moved toward
him. Tom assumed that this movement also was under his control, and
he reached out to repeat it. To his surprise, he wasn't able to feel the
moving thing, much less to control it. Continuing to reach for it, he
managed to get out of bed and walk a couple of precarious steps toward
it. Finally he felt it, gave it a spirited push, and was happy to see that it
moved. All three doctors now converged on him, and Tom quickly
learned one of life's basic facts: that there were other things in existence outside himself, and they expected to have some control over him.
Surprised when the doctors seized him and began forcing him back to
the bed, he at first put up very little resistance. He recovered quickly,
however, and soon was engaged in a very enjoyable fracas, reveling in
the enormous strength which amazed Thomas on later reflection as
much as it did the doctors at the time.

He didn't at all like being tied down in the bed: he had just discovered his power of mobility, and now it was denied him. After the doctors left, however, others released him from his bonds. Relieved to
learn that the non-self world was populated also by individuals with
more kindly dispositions, he made no attempt to renew the battle but
rather contented himself with peacefully observing the passing scene.
Among other things, he noticed that these busy individuals communi-
cated with one another by making sounds, and then listening, to each
other, and he found himself eager to join in the process, if only to reassure them of his own pacific nature and good intentions. For all his
disabilities, he obviously was learning fast.

It had been a full day. As he lay restfully in bed, his exhaustion
overcame him, and he fell asleep for the night.

Next morning he tried to talk. His mouth had not forgotten how to articulate words, but he didn't know their meaning, and the best he could do was to repeat the phrases he heard. Since this merely puzzled the people to whom he was addressing himself, he soon gave up in frustration and turned his attention instead to his growing hunger. It was an unpleasant sensation that he hadn't experienced before, and he didn't know what to do about it. Fortunately the others did, and before long he was brought some breakfast. Although he couldn't identify hunger, he quickly learned how to satisfy it, with a good deal of help from his friends. Having once learned, he was very eager to continue the process, but his voracity rather alarmed his providers, and for the next day or two his greatest inconvenience, as Thomas later put it, "was from hunger and the inability to state the need."

After what seemed an unconscionable lapse of time, one of his friends finally caught on to the fact that, although unable to talk, he could *learn* to talk, and so she began to teach him. She started with the word "apple." After repeating the word after her a few times, he connected it with the object she held in her hand, and was rewarded for his insight by being taught to eat the apple. Her own insight, however, proved to be rather limited, for she failed to recognize that by "apple" he simply meant "food." He naturally asked for "apple" whenever he was hungry, and the response of his friends was such that for a while he had to subsist on a rather unbalanced diet. He liked apples, but this was ridiculous.

Tom's relearning of the language was rapid; once he learned the meaning of a word, he didn't forget it. But there were problems. Although concrete nouns and verbs were fairly easy to learn, abstract nouns and verbs, and other parts of speech like prepositions, proved hard for the teacher to illustrate and the learner to absorb. One can imagine the difficulties presented by the deceptively simple word "fast," which acts as four different parts of speech and has a myriad of meanings. The personal pronouns caused considerable confusion, since the teacher pointed to Tom while saying "you," and it took some doing thereafter to keep him from referring to himself as "you." He also was confused at times by being taught phrases instead of single words, making it necessary for him to backtrack. After being told, for instance, that a black hen was a "black hen," without his having seen a hen before, he identified a white hen as a "white blackhen." In general, however, the setbacks were minor, and the learning, or relearning, proceeded at a reasonably satisfying pace for all concerned.

Much of the process was carried on while he was kept in his sick-bed (not so much from necessity, one suspects, as from oversolicitude), and as a result he was at first unable to accept himself as a person, as one of the "people" he saw about him. Someone finally mentioned that he soon would be up and about, just like other people, and his immediate reaction was one of curiosity as to whether he would wear a dress or a coat and trousers. On the more intimate details concerning this difference the Rev. Thomas Hanna did not elaborate in his report.

The passage of time was a puzzle to him, but then it's a puzzle to the rest of us too. After much study of eagerly presented watches, he managed to arrive at the rudimentary understanding generally consid-ered normal, and this of course was sufficient for practical purposes. A much harder thing to adjust to was the notion of distance, or perspec-tive. At the very beginning, as we have seen, he had no idea of it what-soever. He began to have an inkling of it as his world expanded to arm's length, but it was limited to his sickroom so long as he was in bed. The windows were like pictures (often moving pictures), without reference to an "outside," and the people who left the room were sim-ply annihilated until recreated upon reentering the room. After a while he did grasp the idea that their existence was not interrupted during their absence, but the best explanation he could come up with at first—especially since he found that a person usually would reappear if asked for by name—was that everyone not in the room must be waiting just outside the door. Although he was told that certain people lived so many "miles" away and that others lived "in town," he dismissed all such information as simply incomprehensible.

On the third morning, Saturday, his headache was gone. Since it had been with him from the beginning, he had assumed that it was a normal part of being alive. The pain had been quite intense—Thomas later described it as feeling like "a great weight of hot metal on the head"—and Tom was very happy to learn that it was not to be his con-stant companion. From this time on, when the headache returned tem-porarily, he knew enough to complain about it, so that he would be given something to relieve it.

As he gradually learned the language, people began telling him of his "former life." His first reaction was total disbelief. His friends, however, hit upon a couple of ways to persuade him. When he hap-pened to ask why his hands were darker than the rest of his body, they seized the opportunity to explain that this was due to sunlight. He therefore must have worn clothing, like other men, to protect his body from the sun. They also brought him a photograph of himself wearing clothes. This didn't mean very much to him until they brought him a mirror. Even then the identification process was not an easy one—the mirror alone created some problems—but eventually he was convinced.

With this new information he became insistent on getting out of bed and trying his legs. Although his first steps were very precarious, he didn't fall. He tottered around the room triumphantly for a while and even headed for an adjoining room, but at this point his friends persuaded him that he ought to get back to bed. He agreed, although he could barely contain his curiosity about that other room.

Over the next few days his curiosity was satisfied about more than the other room. That other room, in fact, was rather a disappointment, despite some unfamiliar kinds of furniture. The great outdoors, however, was anything but a disappointment. Before it had been merely pictures on the wall, pictures that he could somehow reach into without touching anything. Now, as he stepped out onto the front porch, it was an overwhelming panorama. The porch itself, extending the length of the house and bare of any carpeting, was something of a surprise. Then there were the front steps, which he negotiated with nervous caution. And finally there was the front lawn. As he put his foot down on the strange green carpet, he found that it was soft, that it yielded under his weight. He withdrew his foot in some alarm, feeling that the ground would not support him. After much reassurance from his friends, who stepped out on it with confidence and without mishap, he took the plunge, and soon he was reveling in the joys of walking on the grass.

He reached out for some of the trees in the distance. No, his friends explained, you'll have to walk quite a way toward them before you can touch them. With their help he did so, and the vastness of the world began to dawn on him. He was eager to explore it, but his friends restrained him with a promise that he could do so before very long.

Although he had some comprehension of the difference between life and nonlife, the subtler distinctions took a lot of explaining. He could see that the trees and the bushes, and even the clouds, could move. Yet such things were not, he was told, like the animals and human beings that moved about him. As for the clouds (thunderheads, apparently), they were lifeless but were "boiling"; this caused some difficulty later, when he was shown some boiling water.

He was told of the impermanence of life, and this distressed him because the world was so full of such marvelous things. Although he

had no fear or understanding of death, he could accept the idea that
he might have to return to the oblivion from which he had emerged
so recently, but he accepted it with great reluctance. He was comforted,
however, by his feeling that, having been reborn at least once, he would
probably be reborn many times again.

Some days after his rebirth he heard some music for the first time,
and this became a new passion. His favorites were hymns, not for their
words but for their melodies, which sometimes could reduce him to
tears. He proved to be an unerring musical critic, always catching a
wrong note or a false tone. He also proved to be a surprisingly good
performer. When a friend brought along a banjo for a singfest one day,
Tom managed—although he had never played a banjo before, in either
life—to learn how to play three songs, none of which he had ever heard.
One of his amazed friends had him watch as he played the piano, and,
after listening and watching for a while, Tom played the piece quite
competently, simply through imitation.

He learned to read and write very rapidly, despite some distress
over the many forms of the alphabet—upper and lowercase, Roman
and script, and so on. His memory for words and their meanings was
phenomenal, at least by ordinary learning standards. As for his writing, his friends were surprised to find that he could write as well with
one hand as the other, though with neither could he write as well as
Thomas Hanna had been able to.

As he grew stronger, both physically and mentally, the doctors permitted him ever greater freedom in walking about the countryside, until finally he was allowed to walk, alone, almost anywhere he wished.
One day, while walking by a pond filled with croaking frogs, he experienced his first dim recollection of his former life. It was like a dream,
hazy and remote, in which he was lying in a carriage while a man,
whom he knew as his brother, feverishly rubbed his hands and his
cheeks. In the background he could hear the croaking of frogs. Then
he seemed to fall asleep, and the recollection ended. None of this
meant anything to him. When he told the doctors about the experience,
however, they were extremely interested. It was, they told him, almost
certainly a memory of events connected with his accident.

Perhaps as a result, they decided that he should be taken to New
York to see some specialists. The train trip and the city itself were
sources for a continuing series of new and astonishing sights and sounds.
The dizzying speed of the train, the city's tall buildings and crowded
streets, the ocean and the ships upon it, all filled his mind to bursting.

His faithful brother, who was accompanying him, could hardly keep up with his questions.

The two specialists whom the doctors at home had recommended were extremely interested in his case, visiting him regularly at the home where he and his brother were staying. Their first efforts were directed toward restoring as much memory as possible of his former life. These efforts, however, despite his own eager attempts to cooperate, proved futile. He had no recollection whatsoever of life before the accident (he thought of the one minor exception as a dream rather than a recollection); the names and places which they brought up to him as connected with that life were quite meaningless to him. Further, since his memory had been so flawless in his secondary state, he had no clear notion of what it meant to forget anything.

The doctors, though impressed by his power of apparently total recall, suspected that it could not be absolutely perfect. They decided to put it to the test in the hope that, if they did find something that he had forgotten, they could point it out to him and thus give him the conscious experience of having forgotten something. Given this experience, perhaps he could come closer to recognizing his long-term memory lapses for what they were.

The first part of this ingenious scheme worked. There were some things that Tom had forgotten, and now, for the first time, he was made conscious of having forgotten a fact or event in the ordinary way. This experience, Thomas testified later, made a deep impression on him, but by no means deep enough to throw a clear light on his former existence. And so the doctors resorted to hypnosis.

His hypnotic dreams were very vivid, very detailed scenes from his former life. The doctors triggered the dreams by suggesting people, places and things from his life before the accident. One striking instance of this procedure had to do with his memory of Hebrew verses. The Rev. Thomas Hanna knew Hebrew, and when the doctors read some Hebrew verses to Tom, he was able to complete them. How he could do this, he didn't know; he "felt as if they were being spoken by another mind using my tongue."

The procedure continued for a long time without any visible results, but it must have had some sort of attritional effect. One morning he awoke about 4:00, after a restful night's sleep. But the "he" who awoke was not Tom, but Thomas. He stared at his surroundings in utter bewilderment. He remembered—rather vaguely, as one does remember casual events—that he had gone home in the carriage with his brother the night before, and he should be in his own bedroom at home this morning. But by no stretch of the imagination was this his own bedroom at home. Springing up from the bed in a panic, he rushed to the other bed and shook its occupant awake. When the occupant turned and looked at him, sleepily and rather grumpily, he recognized his brother and demanded an explanation of his, or their, predicament. After a brief exchange his brother, remarkably, guessed what must have happened. Asking Thomas to remain as calm as he could and promising an explanation shortly, he called one of the doctors, who came right over. The two of them patiently explained the situation, but of course Thomas wasn't having any, thank you. Certainly he of all people would remember the accident, and he didn't. This must be some sort of elaborate practical joke, and he really couldn't see the humor in it. It evidently was quite a scene, with the doctor busily taking notes, the brother dancing about in jubilant relief, and Thomas at his wit's ends trying to make out what was really going on.

With some questioning, Thomas had to admit that he recalled getting his foot caught in the blanket on the floor of the carriage, and this recollection introduced a little uncertainty into his heated protests. Then someone pointed out that there was a way of demonstrating that this was not the morning of April 16 (whether it was the brother or the doctor is not recorded). Thomas was shown a watch reading 4:15 and then shown that the sun was coming up. Since he knew that it would still be dark in April, he had to confess that he must have lost a month or so.

Perhaps this sudden realization was too much for him. Whatever the reason, he sat down on his bed, then lay back on it, and went sound asleep. Afraid to wake him, his brother and the doctor waited for about half an hour, when he showed signs of revival, and then woke him. And now the "him" was Tom again, not Thomas.

By now the other doctor had arrived, and for the rest of the day the three men attended Thomas-Tom as he alternated between sleeping and waking and between the two personalities, or states. While in the primary state, Thomas knew nothing about what had happened while he, Tom, was in the secondary state—and vice versa. In each state he firmly resolved to be helpful to the doctors and to remember what happened—yet in the other state he couldn't even remember the resolution.

The doctors turned their efforts to keeping him awake at all costs. They spelled each other, hammering away at him with recollections from one state to the other, trying desperately to bring the two together. After several hours of this insistent therapy, an ordeal for all concerned, Thomas began seeing glimpses of Tom's life. The doctors, thus encouraged, redoubled their efforts despite their weariness and their patient's near exhaustion. As evening fell, Tom's headache returned. He was beginning to buckle under the persistent harassment. He was aware of no signs of improvement, and the doctors, it seemed, were merely being obstinate now in not giving up the battle. Yet he continued to cooperate, if resentfully, as the evening wore on. Thomas, on the other hand, had grown quite buoyant, emerging ever more strongly and frequently. His glimpses of Tom's life became clear, sustained recollections. The two lives continued to meld into one until finally Thomas, by what he later described as "a deliberate, voluntary act," brought them together for good, in both senses of the word.

Over the next few months Thomas still had to reorganize some of his and Tom's memories—Tom, of course, was not seen again—to get them into the proper sequence for his own emotional security and "so as to present a continuous history." Before the year was out he had everything in order and was a whole man once again.

Mary Vaughn, 1905

From the standpoint of evidence, the case of Mary Vaughn is probably the least satisfactory of those on record. The report, presented by
Drs. H.P. Frost and Boris Sidis in the latter's *Multiple Personality* (Appleton, 1905), is uneven at best, with tantalizing gaps in the information given. Yet the case is included here because it is unique: Mary
Vaughn was insane. Certifiably, as they say.

There were no indications of mental aberrations in her family's
history, but her mother often had frightful temper tantrums, with her
wrath directed at Mary more often than not. During these tantrums she
would beat the child and then thrust her out of doors, regardless of the
weather. Somehow Mary survived this maternal regimen—the father
seems to have been largely a zero quantity, although the children were
fond of him—until she was about thirteen. One evening, plagued by an
extremely severe cold, she fell into a restless, moaning sleep from which
she could not be awakened for several hours. She began having convulsions, and her condition became so alarming that the family doctor put
her in a nearby hospital, where she stayed for over a year under treatment for "epilepsy with mental disturbance."

Although her condition improved enough for her to be discharged
as cured, the effects of the treatment were not very lasting. Five
months after her discharge she was having epileptic seizures again, to
some extent in conjunction with her menstrual periods. During these
attacks she had to be restrained from injuring herself in various ways,
such as repeatedly hitting her head against a wall. Afterward she would
remember nothing that had happened.

People were institutionalized much less readily eighty years ago
than they are today. It was not until July, 1891, when she was 22, that
she was admitted to New York's Buffalo State Hospital suffering from
convulsions in which she was almost catatonic, with her body sometimes engaged in furious activity which included many attempts at suicide. Between attacks she seemed to revert to her childhood, sitting on

the floor and playing with dolls, responding very pleasantly and cooperatively to the approaches and suggestions of the doctors and nurses, and displaying no memory whatsoever of anything that had happened during any of the seizures.

The hospital notes on her case indicated nothing more peculiar about it until July, 1893. On the 12th of that month she went into a series of convulsions that lasted until the 26th, and this time she emerged from her last seizure remembering nothing at all about the whole period, including the times between attacks. Further, she behaved differently between the attacks, being much more irascible and abusive than she had ever been before. On the 26th she seemed to revert to her former self, asking many questions about the events of the two missing weeks and greeting a nurse who had returned from leave in quite the same way as she had greeted her on July 9th.

From this point on the hospital notes referred more and more often to the patient's "two personalities" and "different states." In November, 1894, she first reported hearing the voice of a nagging old woman who, later identified as a recollection of her mother, was to remain with her from that time on. Over the next five years her seizures were generally accompanied by changes in personality, sometimes distinct and sometimes blurred. In general, one personality was well—well enough on occasion to go home for a visit—and the other was sick, although this was an uneasy generalization at best. Neither personality knew anything about the other, except at second hand. Neither had any of the other's memories: one remembered the father's death, for example, and the other remembered a brother's death, but neither remembered both. Yet on rare occasions one would recollect an event experienced by the other. Each was terrified by the personality changes.

On January 8, 1900, Mary Vaughn was referred to the two doctors, Frost and Sidis, who studied her condition for the next three weeks. She passed the preliminary tests very handily: temperature, pulse, pupil reactions, muscular reflexes, kinesthetic and tactile sensations, and so on—everything was quite normal. But she displayed an abnormal fear of the doctors and their instruments, and she complained of pain without specifying any location. Her understanding of time ranged from primitive to nonexistent. She "felt" as though she might be in her middle fifties but confessed that she really had no idea of how old she was. She didn't know what her name was because it changed so often, but "they call me Mary." She was functionally illiterate or worse, being

able to read only simple phrases in a familiar handwriting, and to write
not at all.

She was very responsive to the questions put to her. She could remember being "more than one person" for about as long as she had
been at the state hospital (nine years). The others were somehow in
herself, including the old woman, whom she now could hear talking to
her with never a moment's respite. Most of the time she couldn't understand what the old woman was saying. What she did understand was
invariably unpleasant and, the old woman demanded, was not to be repeated. Mary obeyed, for she was dimly yet firmly convinced that this
was her mother speaking. But it was her mother as she had been more
than forty years before.

The influence of Mary's psychotic condition could perhaps be seen
most clearly in her answers to questions about the various personalities.
Her responses were quite vague and even incoherent; the doctors had to
do a great deal of backing and filling before arriving at what they felt
was a reasonably accurate picture of what she was saying. Over the past
hundred years, she testified, she had lived four lives and was now living
her fifth. A century ago she had been an Irish roughneck named Mike
Muckey, who lived a life of petty crime and who finally drank himself
to death. He nevertheless must have lived to a ripe old age, since according to her testimony he had died, in prison, rather recently.

In her second life her name was Jennie Longnecker, who evidently
led a very proper and uneventful life. Perhaps for contrast, she was followed by Jesse James—none other than *the* Jesse James, the Robin
Hood of the Golden West—who in turn was followed by the innocuous
Mary Vaughn. Mary Vaughn was now dead, she stoutly insisted against
the unanimous testimony of friends and relatives, and she was now living as a fifth personality, so far nameless. The doctors, suspecting that
all this might be a scenario dreamed up for their benefit on the spur of
the moment, made some inquiries among the hospital attendants and
were assured that these delusions were of quite long standing. One
nurse recalled the same stories being told six years earlier. She also recalled—and this the doctors later verified—that in her more lucid moments Mary had told of knowing a man named Mike Muckey and of
having a friend named Jennie Longnecker long before her admission to
the hospital.

As the days passed, the old woman became stronger and more garrulous. She talked throughout the day. Mary could never completely
divorce herself from the ceaseless monologue. Sometimes she could be

distracted from it by being shown something new to her, but never fully distracted and never for long. Throughout each night she whispered and muttered unceasingly, evidently in some consonance with the old woman's monologue (although she would never admit doing this). Her role as captive audience of one was rendered particularly painful by severe earaches, usually in both ears, during which the din from the old woman was especially excruciating. When she was examined by an ear specialist, however, everything—drum membranes, air and bone conduction, hearing acuity, and so on—was found to be perfectly normal. Shortly after that examination, on the same day, she was given some word-association tests; her responses were dominated by obsessive references to her mother.

The records ends rather abruptly on February 1. Although the doctors thought that there had been some improvement in terms of personality stability, Mary was still hearing the old woman, was still whispering and muttering. They must have considered her case hopeless, or at least much less promising than many or most of the others demanding their attention. It probably can be assumed that Mary Vaughn spent the rest of her life in an institution.

Christine Beauchamp, 1905

In American medical history there have been three major, widely reported and widely discussed cases of multiple personality. The first of these occurred in the early part of the twentieth century. Dr. Morton Prince, a Harvard-educated physician who taught at the Tuft's College Medical School in addition to his practice, was intensely interested in the new developments in psychology, including the use of hypnotism as a therapeutic tool. (He later founded the highly respected *Journal of Abnormal and Social Psychology*.) One of his patients was a hospital nurse who had suffered a "nervous breakdown" as a result of the pressures of her profession, and whom we shall call Mary Beauchamp. He reported her case in *The Dissociation of a Personality* (Longmans, Green, 1905).

Miss Beauchamp was an extremely inhibited person with deep religious feelings and high ethical standards. As might be expected of someone like this, she was much too shy to feel at ease in discussing her emotional problems even with a good friend, much less a total stranger. To dissipate or at least reduce her tense diffidence, Dr. Prince suggested trying hypnosis, and she agreed. Although the hypnosis did not bring on anything like a complete transformation, she was much more relaxed in the hypnotic state, less inhibited and less reluctant to talk about herself. After a few sessions with the doctor, indeed, her health and outlook seemed to be improving.

And then one day the doctor was startled to realize that she was referring to herself in the third person in describing one of her experiences—"she" did this, "she" felt that, and so on. Further, he noticed differences in the way she looked and moved and spoke, as though she were imitating some other person. Who, he asked her, was this "she"? The question seemed to confuse her. It's you, he suggested; you are this "she." No, no, she remonstrated, she doesn't know what I know, she doesn't have the same thoughts. But you have the same body! Yes, but that doesn't make us the same person! And so it went, with the doctor finally losing the argument. Yet in their next session a few days later the young woman, again under hypnosis, denied quite stoutly that any such thing could have happened. The doctor awakened her and put her to sleep again, and this time she clearly recalled the incident. After a few such alternating denials and affirmations, the doctor began to accept that he was dealing with two different personalities.

A peculiarity that he had noticed while Mary was under hypnosis was that she rubbed her eyes a great deal. Although he tried to discourage this habit, he attached no particular significance to it, assuming that it was simply a symptom of her nervousness. During a conversation with the other personality, however, he learned that it was she who was doing the eye-rubbing because, she explained, she wanted to "get her eyes open." Alarmed by this information, he redoubled his efforts to discourage the practice, fearing that if the second personality did manage to "get her eyes open" she would thereafter be able to assert her existence more freely and thus aggravate Mary's problems.

This is exactly what happened. Not long afterward, at home, Mary became excited over something and the second personality emerged. Without the doctor there to discourage her, she rubbed her eyes until indeed she got them open, and from then on she could emerge at will. As time passed, she became an ever more assertive and independent personality, privy to all of Mary's thoughts and even able to control her behavior at times. Unlike Mary, she was carefree and mischievous. She chose her name quite capriciously, for example, from a book she happened to like, and from that time on she was known as Sally.

Mary Beauchamp had not been a completely ordinary child. Although Dr. Prince apparently never learned much about her family or her home life, he did discover that her deep religious feelings extended far back into her childhood and included a number of mystical experiences. Whenever she found herself in some uncomfortable predicament, for instance, she usually could summon up a vision of Jesus Christ and his mother Mary for a solution to her problem or at least for reassurance that it would not prove insurmountable. They were very real to her and were a recurrent source of comfort.

Evidently there were two great passions in her life. One was her intense ambition to be a hospital nurse, an ambition perhaps not matched by the requisite degree of emotional stability. She managed to qualify herself and had accumulated several years' experience when Dr. Prince first met her. The other passion in her life was a man whom she had known as a child. Much older and more sophisticated than she, he seems to have assumed the proportions of an unattainable but absorbingly desirable god. Although she had seen very little of him over the past few years, she had never forgotten him.

One evening about six years before her first visit to Dr. Prince, Mary was chatting with a friend, another nurse, in a second-floor sitting room at the hospital. It had been a rough evening for her. An especially severe thunderstorm had been raging outside earlier, so that her nerves were on edge to begin with. Then one of the mental patients had become delirious and rather violent, and this unsettling experience had made her very jumpy indeed. As she rested in the sitting room trying to recover, a face unexpectedly appeared at one of the windows. This alone might have been startling enough to shock her, but the real shock came in her recognition of the face as that of her old friend and hero from her younger days.

The shock evidently was profound, even though she soon learned that her friend had merely yielded to a prankish impulse. Stopping off on his way to New York, he had come to the hospital, had noticed a ladder left against the wall (apparently by some workmen at quitting time), and had climbed up to the window to look in. The explanation was not enough to calm Mary down. For several days she stayed at a high level of agitation, pacing the wards and walking about the hospital grounds instead of sleeping and relaxing during her off-duty hours. And, although this turmoil within her gradually subsided, her general, long-term nervousness and excitability grew slowly but steadily worse. It is small wonder that Dr. Prince, in diagnosing her condition after her first visit, described her as seriously neurasthenic.

Over most of the next seven years of treatment, the doctor found no reason to substantially modify his initial diagnosis. Although the emergence of Sally Beauchamp, and her increasingly frequent dominance, provided Mary with an avenue of release from her most trying moments, the latter paid a heavy price. Sally thoroughly disliked Mary ("I hate her, Dr. Prince!"), and, since she knew all her thoughts and feelings and could often control her actions, she was distressingly able and sadistically willing to indulge in tricks that would make her miserable. Of the two personalities, however, Dr. Prince considered Sally much the healthier. Mary was better educated—unlike Sally, for instance, she could speak French and write shorthand—but she was pathologically "religious," morbidly scrupulous, anxiety-ridden, generally depressed and not infrequently in pain. In contrast, Sally (who was never in pain) was fun-loving, carefree, buoyantly irreligious, bright, lively, saucy, and in general most attractively cheerful. Yet her character was marred by the cruelty she exhibited in her treatment of Mary.

Within a few weeks of her first emergence—she dated events, incidentally, as before or after the day when she "got her eyes open"—Sally was able to "come out" for hours and even days at a time. At first she usually would emerge in response to an unconscious distress call from Mary, but it wasn't long before Mary lost even this control over these experiences, which to her of course were simply blackouts. And it was partly during these blackouts that Sally would play her rather nasty practical jokes.

A particularly nasty one, for example, involved a small collection of snakes and spiders. Knowing that Mary was terrified of both, she went out into the country one day, gathered up a supply of the animals, and put them in a little box. Back home, she wrapped the box very tastefully, addressed it to "Miss Beauchamp," and left it on a table. When Mary emerged, she opened the package and of course almost went out of her mind. Although none of the creatures was poisonous, they were extremely loathsome to her, and the ensuing hunt was especially unnerving because she had to handle the ones most reluctant to leave.

On some other occasions Sally would hire a hack to take her out of town and deep into the countryside. Passing a gate to some remote, thoroughly isolated farm, she would ask to be let out on some pretext, such as that she could walk the rest of the way. After the hack was out of sight, she would toss away whatever money she had left and than wake up Mary, who thus would find herself forced to walk or hitchhike back to town. These experiences were exhausting and embarrassing, and they did nothing to settle her nerves.

Another trick of Sally's was especially frustrating. A friend of Mary's had asked her to knit a blanket for a recently arrived baby, and Mary had gladly agreed. It turned out to be quite a project, taking almost a year to complete, for, whenever Mary had the blanket nearly finished, Sally would take over and unravel it. After going through this sisyphean experience several times, Mary finally emerged from a blackout one day to discover herself in a great web of unraveled yarn. In sweeping whorls and hopeless snarls, the yarn was wound around the chairs, the tables, the bed, even the pictures on the wall—and around Mary herself, who had to cut her way out of the woolly chaos.

Sally did not limit her acts of harassment to the use of blackout periods. At times she would actually take over Mary's will power, with

Mary still fully conscious, and make her do painfully humiliating things. She would attack Mary's over-developed sense of decorum, for example, by making her sit with her feet up on the mantelpiece, in a sprawling position that would be considered gauche even in our relaxed times. Despite her great mortification, Mary could do nothing about the situation until Sally, relenting, allowed her to regain her dignity and composure.

Another area in which Mary was vulnerable to Sally's mischievous pranks was her dedication to telling the truth. To Mary, telling even a half-truth or a white lie was sinful. So Sally would have her tell outrageous lies. On one occasion, asked who lived in a hovel at the edge of town, Mary heard herself replying with the name of a well-known and very wealthy dowager. But, her companion remonstrated, isn't she extremely rich? Oh, Mary was compelled to reply, she lost all her money and was reduced to these circumstances. The dowager actually, of course, was living quite comfortably in her elaborate mansion elsewhere in the town, and Sally was aware that both Mary and the questioner knew this—and that Mary knew that the questioner knew it. On another occasion she caused Mary to tell a wild story about a new baby in the neighborhood, to the effect that it didn't have a bone in its body and was kept precariously alive with a special diet of oatmeal. It's not hard to imagine Mary's horror at hearing herself say such things and at seeing the expressions on her listeners' faces.

Such malicious pranks were by no means Sally's only means of making her victim's life miserable. At times she would take control of the available money—which she could hide from Mary, of course, but which Mary could never hide from her—and would dole out some meager allowance, like five cents a day. In the morning Mary would find the nickel or five pennies on a table, usually with a note explaining that this was her spending money for the day and cautioning her against going into debt. Often, too, she would discover that her supply of postage stamps had disappeared. On these occasions, if she wrote a letter, she would have to leave it on the desk; later she would find a stamp affixed to the envelope, but only if Sally approved her mailing it. Sally's own correspondence with her was quite voluminous: Mary continually found letters awaiting her in the morning, criticizing her character and conduct and regaling her with reports, all quite untrue, of unkind things that people had said about her. Sometimes Sally, in an especially creative mood, would include some malicious doggerel.

Mary's greatest handicap in this unequal battle was her blacking out while Sally was in control, whereas Sally not only was privy to all Mary's thoughts and emotions but also could indulge in her own separate train of thought while fully conscious of Mary's. During one of her early appearances to Dr. Prince, for instance, she smoked a cigarette, something that Mary would never do. In a later interview the doctor remarked to her that Mary on that day, after resuming control, had shown signs of tasting the tobacco-smoke residue in her mouth. Oh, yes, Sally responded in explanation, she thought you must have given her some quinine but was too timid to ask why.

Evidently Sally was free enough even to be inattentive at times, for one day she wasn't sufficiently alert to stop Mary from inadvertently tearing up some paper money instead of a half-written letter. She informed the doctor of this during the next interview, and the doctor in turn informed Mary when she reappeared. She responded by going to her coat to take the money from the pocket—where, of course, she found the letter. She still insisted, however, that she couldn't have destroyed the money, and she seemed only partly convinced even after she had witnessed the act in the doctor's crystal ball.

The doctor often used the crystal-gazing technique, sometimes in conjunction with hypnosis, to reveal a patient's suppressed experiences. (Mary earlier had been shocked to see herself wantonly smoking that cigarette.) But not infrequently he needed Sally's help to interpret a crystal vision. In one of these visions, Mary saw herself get out of a sickbed, pace up and down, climb onto a windowsill, and throw out an inkpot. Although she recognized the room, she could neither recall nor explain the incident. But Sally could, and did. Mary, she explained, was quite ill with pneumonia and had dreamed that she was walking along a seashore. In a delirious sleepwalking trance, she climbed up on a rock (the windowsill) and tossed a stone (the inkpot) out into the water. Sally knew all along not only what Mary had done but also why she had done it.

The doctor continued to work with his patient through the years. She seemed to have periods of improvement and then of relapse; he could never feel confident that there was any long-term trend in either direction. And then one day, as he was about to hypnotize her, the patient remonstrated that only Dr. Prince should do that. Despite his efforts to identify himself, she kept insisting that he was Will, the old friend who had visited her at the hospital in such unconventional fashion, and about whom the doctor knew nothing at this time. The doctor did not press her further to reestablish his identity, but during subsequent interviews she gradually came to accept him and his function. She was, he discovered, a much different personality from either Mary or Sally. This woman, Christine Beauchamp, seemed mentally healthier and more mature than either of the others, and even more knowledgeable, although she could not remember nearly so much of her own early history. Because of her lack of recall, and presumably because of an apprehensive jealousy, Sally called her "The Idiot." (With similar contempt, though without apprehension, she regularly called Mary "The Saint.")

Christine proved very adept at letting herself go in fantasies, and with the doctor's help she was able eventually to reconstruct her past quite fully and accurately. As he worked with her and her condition improved (he never did know just why), he became ever more convinced that she, and not Mary or Sally, was the real person behind the dissociations. Gradually she seemed to absorb the other personalities—usually under hypnosis at first, but the necessity for this slowly diminished as the interviews progressed. Finally the day came when Dr. Prince felt confident that she was cured, and he discharged her. His feeling was justified by events: she suffered no further relapses, and eventually she married and had a family. And, so far as is known, she lived at least much more happily ever after.

Irene, 1907

Irene was a poor French girl whose troubles began shortly before the turn of the century. Her case was reported by a famous psychiatrist, Pierre Janet, in a journal article which he later included in a book, *The Major Symptoms of Hysteria* (Macmillan, 1907). His report unfortunately was quite sketchy, but the case is included here because it was one of the earliest cases observed and because of Dr. Janet's considerable reputation in the history of multiple-personality research and treatment.

The conditions of Irene's life were those of Victor Hugo's Paris, although they might just as easily have been those of Charles Dickens' London. By the time that her case had come to Dr. Janet's attention, her father's increasingly heavy drinking had reduced the family (father, mother and daughter) to the kind of squalid destitution and personal misery commonly associated with the seamier side of the Industrial Revolution. Their wretched garret rang persistently with bitter quarreling between father and daughter while the mother, who was dying of tuberculosis, sat at her primitive sewing machine and worked away in a desperate effort to earn some pittance for the next day's gruel. To a modern, relatively affluent American their situation sounds like a parody. But of course it wasn't a parody.

The strain on Irene evidently brought her to the edge of hysteria, and her mother's death carried her over it. The slow, corrosive approach of death was a harrowing experience for her. For some nine weeks she hovered anxiously about the bedside while her mother gasped ever more weakly for breath and vomited ever smaller quantities of blood. When the end finally came, Irene could not accept it. She tried frantically to bring the body back to life, lifting it from the bed, falling to the floor under its weight, struggling to return it to the bed.

Evidently no one else was present, but this scene came to light in dissociations not long after the funeral. During these dissociations, which sometimes lasted for several hours and which Dr. Janet considered an extreme form of sleepwalking, Irene would reenact the scene of her mother's death in one way or another. Sometimes she would merely sit in her chair and silently watch the scene as it took place in her mind's eye—or so it seemed from her reactions, including eyes wide with terror and then filled with tears, mouth and jaw set tensely, hands gripping the chair arms, and her occasional muted cries. At other times she would accompany such reactions with a verbal account of the scene, describing it in a rushing flow of words and in meticulous detail. And at still other times she would act out the drama while she described it, going through all the motions without any variations between one time and the next. She would discuss things with her mother, speaking to her and listening to her opinions. The subjects of their discussions eventually included her own plans for her death by suicide, and before long she was also enacting a scene in which she lay down on the floor, imagining herself stretched across some railroad tracks. Soon a train would bear down upon her, and she would shriek with pain and fright as it passed over her. After a moment she would get up again and repeat all or some portion of the preceding scene, sometimes as many as four or five times.

Usually it would be simply sheer exhaustion that would bring her back to normal, to her primary self. She would remember nothing that had occurred during the dissociations. Indeed, she remembered nothing about her mother's death. She knew that her mother must be dead, she confessed, only because people had told her so and because her mother was no longer present. But she didn't know what had caused her death, and she was troubled that she hadn't been there to take care of her in her last hours.

The death was deeply shocking to her, and it was a long time before she recovered from it. In fact, there is no clear evidence or testimony that she ever really did.

Doris Fischer, 1915

Consider this scene for a moment. A little girl of four or five is sitting on a living-room floor quietly playing with some toys. She picks up a ball from the floor beside her with her left hand, transfers it to her right hand. Suddenly her face distorts with anger, and with her left hand she scratches viciously at her face, bringing blood to her cheeks and forehead. Then just as suddenly she stops the scratching and sits there crying and talking to herself.

This was Doris Fischer in 1893 or '94. A year or so earlier, she had been thrown to the floor by her drunken, infuriated father during a violent quarrel with her mother. She apparently suffered no permanent physical damage, but psychologically she broke into several pieces. From then on, to her family and friends, she was moody and unpredictable. They never knew what she was going to do next.

Nor, by and large, did she. She could never be sure of her control over her body or her mind, a control now shared precariously with a new playmate named Margaret, a child of her own age who somehow mysteriously existed within her. This other self was usually a delightful companion, but her charmingly impish character was marred by a nasty streak of jealousy. She was very possessive over anything that she considered hers, be it a toy, a doll, a ball. She expected Doris to respect her property rights scrupulously, and her method of enforcement was indiscriminate scratching. After a few experiences with the enforcement procedure, Doris was not only scrupulous but extremely cautious about title to any possessions.

Margaret was not the only secondary personality produced during the quarrel, although she was the only one that Doris knew about. Doris talked in her sleep now, a great deal more than she ever had before. Evidently no one paid any particular attention to her nocturnal monologues, and it was not until she was a young adult that these discourses were discovered to be coming from another, distinct personality, quite different from either Doris or Margaret. The monologues

65

then became dialogues, for this new personality, who came to be known as Sleeping Margaret, was quite willing to answer the questions that were so eagerly put to her. Unlike Doris and Margaret, she was always conscious, always aware of what the others were doing, of what Margaret was thinking, of what was going on around her. Despite her name, sleeping was what she did *not* do.

Sleeping Margaret was no problem for Doris, since she emerged only when Doris was asleep. Unlike Margaret, she was mature and self-controlled, and nothing she ever said was compromising or embarrassing. She never took over muscular control of anything but the face, the only exceptions being the rare occasions when she would sit up for a few moments. If Sleeping Margaret had been the only secondary personality, Doris might well have gone through life without any notice being taken of her behavior, at least beyond some casual comment about her talking in her sleep.

Sleeping Margaret was a great help to Dr. Walter F. Prince, who was most immediately responsible for the treatment of Doris during the last forty months of her illness and who reported the case in 1915 in the *Proceedings of the American Society for Psychical Research.* Prince was a doctor of divinity to whom Doris was brought for help. He was manifestly a man of uncommon intelligence and understanding, with a similarly bright and sympathetic wife. He was very much interested and quite knowledgeable in the new discipline of abnormal psychology and was acquainted with the Christine Beauchamp case as reported by Morton Prince, to whom he evidently was not related.

In working with Doris, he and his wife relied greatly on the advice and help of a friend who was a reputable neurologist. They relied also, as has been suggested, on the advice and help of Sleeping Margaret, who seemed genuinely concerned about Doris's condition from day to day. Although she was not directly aware of Doris's thought processes, but only of Margaret's, she learned a great deal from Margaret about what Doris was thinking and was quite willing to divulge what she had learned to Dr. Prince. It was she who provided him with most of his information on the history of the case, information which he then could check against the recollections of Doris's relatives and friends.

Although these relatives and friends knew nothing of dissociated personalities, they did recall that Doris, from about the age of three, had behaved very erratically, in something like manic-depressive cycles, seeming sometimes puckish and merry, at other times diffident and sober. As Sleeping Margaret later explained it, Doris remained completely submerged for the first three months after that shattering quarrel, yielding the floor (literally, to a great extent) to Margaret. Then, over the next several years, she began to emerge, at first very briefly (often for only a few seconds) but gradually for longer periods and with greater confidence. Once she had learned how to adapt to Margaret's possessiveness, the two seem to have gotten along splendidly most of the time.

In her seventh year Doris had to go to school, and this created a problem for a while. For her part, the settled routine of the school day was quite welcome, but to Margaret it was an intolerable bore. A natural mischief-maker, Margaret reveled in the role of class cutup. Not infrequently she would simply take French leave for as much as an hour or so. On warm days, when the classroom became as stuffy and oppressive as the lessons, she would sometimes return from such forays with her face and hair, and occasionally even her clothes, sopping wet. For the first several months of school she complained continually to Doris about this pernicious practice of daily incarceration, until she finally recognized that Doris couldn't do anything about it and that indeed it was bigger than both of them. Thereafter she stopped her grumbling but persisted in her maverick habits, attending to business only when Doris was called on to do some writing or conjugating of verbs, both of which activities Margaret enjoyed, for some unfathomable reason. In these and the other subjects Doris somehow managed to do quite well, so that she regularly brought home report cards filled with A's and B's but sporting one F, in conduct.

Margaret thus had become something of a Frankenstein's monster: created to fill a need, she had proved very hard to live with. As she grew older, Doris developed considerable skill in dealing with the embarrassing predicaments in which Margaret often left her. Unlike Margaret, she was unconscious when submerged, at least in the sense that she never remembered anything that had happened when Margaret was in control. Since Margaret might decide to recede at any time—in the middle of a conversation with some friends, for instance—Doris had to spend a lot of time and effort casting about in uncertain waters ("I'm sorry, Gladys, but I don't think I understood that last remark," and so on). This continual dissembling, however successful, was at best pretty exhausting. As a child she had received punishment for things she didn't know she had done; as a young girl she received blank stares, puzzled frowns, sly smiles and unbelieving snickers. It was all very trying.

During the first four years of school Doris blacked out for most of every evening. When she emerged from the amnesia she would find dolls and toys strewn about, some of her homework done, and several notes addressed to her in Margaret's handwriting, mostly critical. But about at the end of the fourth year Margaret's mental development was arrested—she never got much beyond the age of ten—while Doris's continued normally. Within a year or so the schoolwork assigned to Doris was utterly beyond Margaret's ability. As a result Margaret lost interest completely, and what little help she had provided now dwindled to zero, but without any reduction in her mischief-making. When it came time for high school, she not only refused to entertain any suggestion that Doris might go; she even kept Doris from going to the graduation exercises for her diploma, lest she get any hifalutin ideas . . . .

And so Doris got herself a job. She was not unhappy about working for wages, since she now could bring money home regularly to her mother, whom she idolized. Margaret continued to give her trouble, however, and with hindsight it seems clear that Doris was on the verge of further dissociation, awaiting only something to trigger it. That trigger came one day when she was seventeen, in the form of shock over her mother's death.

The death was sudden and unexpected. One May morning, after Doris had left for work, her mother began to feel unwell. By the time Doris got home she was in bed, and very sick. By two o'clock the next morning she was dead. Doris managed to hold on long enough to call the doctor and to make the necessary arrangements, but then Margaret took over. This time, however, she lasted only a few moments. As Sleeping Margaret described the situation later, the left side of the head was seized by a piercing pain, Margaret abruptly disappeared, and a new personality, who was to be known as Sick Doris, appeared on the scene.

Now it was Margaret's turn to have a nuisance on her hands. Doris herself was gone, thoroughly absent, and as it turned out would not even begin to come back for two solid months. As for Sick Doris, she had no memory whatsoever, not even of elementary things like the use of a glass or a spoon. She had no vocabulary, active or passive. She moved her arms and legs as though by instinct; she could pick things up, and she could walk. Eating and drinking, however, were things that she had to learn the hard way—hard for Margaret, especially. The same was true of dressing and undressing: at first Sick Doris was under the impression that her clothing was an integral part of her body, an impression that made her as militantly possessive as Margaret. For a while she made no distinction between the animate and inanimate, although movement of any kind fascinated her. Indeed, for the first day or so she had no firm grasp on the distinction between self and other. By and large, she was a brand-new baby in a seventeen-year-old body.

Without much enthusiasm but with a great deal of grim determination, Margaret set about educating her. Through a trial-and-error, say-and-do method (and by working night and day), she succeeded in equipping Sick Doris with a simple working vocabulary in about a week. Her pupil was a quick study, and the learning process took place at a pace enormously faster than would have been possible with a genuine infant, since it was mostly a relearning process, a recalling of memories from the unconscious. This explanation is supported by the fact that Sick Doris before long achieved an adult level of knowledge and competence, which ten-year-old Margaret could not have provided. With Margaret's help for starters, she soon was following Doris's old routine without serious mishaps, going to work each day, doing the housework in her off hours, getting the groceries, preparing the meals, and so on.

Sick Doris, as her name may imply, was not a very attractive person; appealing, perhaps, in a pathetic way, but not attractive as, for example, the impish Margaret was most of the time. She was an impassive type, often lugubrious. She was not as intelligent as Doris nor as fun-loving as Margaret; unlike them, she never found anything funny. In conversation they invited eye contact; she avoided it, as she did physical contact. She spoke largely in a monotone, and somewhat raspingly. She was withdrawn, diffident, nervous, and about as affectionate as a Giacometti sculpture, although she did have friends, partly because she hugely enjoyed making presents for them.

She was the most assiduously pious of the three personalities. Margaret was quite content with being a happy little heathen; going to church and reading the Bible, in her opinion, amounted to doing "dumb stuff." Doris did both these things, but moderately and deliberately, out of intellectual conviction. Sick Doris also did both, but not so moderately and more ritualistically, like someone scrupulously observing the spiritual amenities.

Sick Doris's competence, though generally adequate, was very uneven. There were some quite basic operations that she was never able to fathom; for example, she never learned how to set a clock or watch. Yet in other things her skill was breathtaking; she embroidered, for instance, not only with great artistry but at an almost unbelievable pace.

One time, in connection with some sort of contest, she finished a complicated piece of embroidery in twelve hours which the judges had expected to take forty-eight. She completed it, furthermore, in one sitting, the only interruptions being cataleptic seizures of ten minutes or so during which she sat rigidly in her chair, eyes glazed, needle in upraised hand. As might be expected, when the work resumed she was quite unaware of the attack. Such exhibitions of her virtuosity were not infrequent and usually were capped by a performance that must have been startling to the uninitiated, when Margaret celebrated completion of the task with an exuberant victory dance.

For the next five years, from age 17 to 22, Sick Doris was the dominant personality. She was often replaced by Margaret, however, especially when she was tired or distressed over some unpleasantness. Sleeping Margaret was active, too, providing some measure of continuity if not stability. But Doris herself was almost completely submerged, appearing for only a few minutes at a time. In those five years, Dr. Prince later estimated, she probably was "on deck" for a total of less than 75 hours.

One morning some 15 months after the mother's death, Margaret fell down some stairs, suffering a severe blow on the head. That night a fifth and final personality emerged, another sleep-talker, whom Margaret dubbed Sleeping Real Doris chiefly because she talked somewhat as Doris might have been expected to talk in her sleep. Yet at other times she spoke quite differently, in a distinct and much more unpleasant voice and with facial expressions quite unlike Doris's. Throughout her existence she stayed in the shadows, never fully formed, always in a state of some bewilderment. One could hardly blame her.

When Sick Doris came to Dr. Prince for help in the late autumn of 1910, when she was twenty, he accepted her as a troubled but single personality. Even on her first visit, however, her behavior changes were frequent and radical enough for him to suspect that he was dealing with some sort of split or dual personality, and after a few more visits his suspicion deepened into conviction. Her home life, he soon learned, was sufficiently miserable to severely strain a vulnerable personality: the mother's death had left an enduring void, and life with father was very difficult at best. (Among his first experiences with Margaret was her repeated cry, "Daddy, don't hit me!")

Finding Sick Doris pathetic and her condition fascinating, he and his wife invited her to visit them whenever she felt the urge, and soon she was doing so quite regularly. By the end of the year he had begun keeping a diary on the case, from which of course he later wrote his journal article.

The entry for Sunday, January 22, 1911, reports a day of crisis. There were three visits that day. In the morning Sick Doris arrived with a complaint that she had awakened with scratches on her arms and on one hip, which was bleeding. After receiving first aid and some badly needed sympathy, she returned home.

That afternoon Margaret put in an appearance, obviously in a playful mood. Would she, Dr. Prince asked, like to tease him? Oh, yes, she replied in delight. Very well, do so, he countered, but leave Sick Doris alone. Margaret's attitude changed immediately. Her grin was replaced by a scowl. Her response was firm and monosyllabic: No! She departed fuming.

That evening the Princes' visitor was Sick Doris, who arrived looking very tired and dispirited. To their efforts at conversation she responded only with weary monosyllables, and soon she was curled up on a sofa, fast asleep. Margaret emerged shortly in one of her fouler moods and began scratching viciously at the neck and the left hip. Dr. Prince tried to stop this activity, of course, but her strength and agility were too much for him. Desperately, he decided to try the power of suggestion. In a loud, deep voice that he hoped she would find impressive, he began making the kind of statements associated with hypnosis— "I am taking away your strength," "You're growing weaker, weaker," and so on. It worked, or something did. Her efforts at resistance did grow steadily weaker, until finally he was able to say, "your strength is gone," for the resistance stopped altogether, the facial expression altered, and the body came awake as Sick Doris.

The real crisis was just beginning. Sick Doris had awakened in a state of extreme lethargy. She could speak only haltingly, with great effort. She also seemed to be drifting into a coma, and the Princes feared that she might be dying. He felt her pulse; it was weak and had dropped to 54. In a few moments she was so quiet that Dr. Prince bent down over her face to see whether he could detect any breath.

He was startled to hear a voice coming from her telling him that she was in danger ("She is," not "I am") and must be brought out of her apathy at once. Fearful that she could prove to be a victim of amateur hypnosis, he began shaking her, at first gently and then roughly, while the voice urged him on to even greater effort. When she failed to respond, the voice demanded that the Princes walk her up and down until she was revived. This wasn't easy, for she had gone quite limp, but they managed to stagger around with her until the voice assured them that she was coming back and soon would be all right.

This proved to be true enough, except that they couldn't make out *who* was all right. What they did observe was that Sick Doris and Margaret were alternately in control. For the initial 30 or 40 minutes the alternations (and alterations) were very rapid, averaging perhaps two per minute and clearly manifested by changes in what the two personalities said, how they said it, and how they looked when they said it. Meanwhile, the body was growing freer of the lassitude that had seized it, first relaxing in the feet and legs, then in the hands and arms, until finally Margaret was able to go on the attack again. Restraining her this time was easier, however, and after a while she dropped into a deep sleep, from which Sick Doris awoke in time to go home and make breakfast for her father. It was five o'clock in the morning.

On the following evening Sick Doris came back, once again weary and laconic. She did have enough energy, nevertheless, to complain that the one thing she had asked of God was the very thing that He refused her, to be released from this life. Had she, asked Dr. Prince, ever prayed for the departure of the voices she heard? The question seemed to give her intense pain. No, she replied. Dr. Prince persisted, recommending that she at least try that approach. The pain seemed to increase, her face changed, and Margaret angrily remonstrated with him. Do you, he asked, fear prayer? Yes. Can it weaken you? Yes. He thereupon said a prayer, aloud, and Margaret went quietly to sleep. (She has gone away for now, Sleeping Margaret explained.) After about twenty minutes, Dr. Prince called on her to wake up. She did so, with a beautiful smile that he found totally unfamiliar. After it had disappeared, Sleeping Margaret explained that he had met the real Doris for the first time. She had appeared for only a moment, and now Sick Doris was back. After making sure that she felt well enough, he sent her home.

Sending her home, the doctor soon concluded, was hazardous to her mental health. He had some hope that she might be cured, but only if she could be freed from her tense and oppressive home environment. Early in March, as he phrased it in his journal report, he "wrung from the father a reluctant and entirely heartless consent for his daughter to live for a while with the family which she was destined never to leave." That family, of course, was the Princes', and the effect of the move was immediate. On the following day Doris herself appeared long enough to be told of the move, and she received the news with astonishment and undiluted joy. Thereafter, very gradually, she began emerging more often and for longer periods. Sick Doris began to weaken. Her memories began to fade and to merge with Doris's, and Margaret complained that she could no longer get through to her.

As Sick Doris grew weaker, the real Doris grew stronger. On March 10 she spent the entire night in the emerged state, for the first time in over 17 years. By the 16th, Sick Doris clearly was losing the power of her five senses, especially of taste and smell. She was permitted to do housework but was not allowed to do any sewing because of the likelihood of cataleptic seizures. This restriction must have been a severe blow to her, since sewing was what she lived for. By early April she could no longer remember what her father's house looked like or how to get there; nor could she recall any incidents of the immediately preceding day. She grew ever more childlike and lethargic as her memory waned. By April 10 she no longer recognized Dr. Prince, calling him "Mister" and pleading with him (for she sensed what was happening) not to let her disappear. By the 21st she no longer knew her own name.

Her sense of taste and smell having long since departed, in early May her vision began to go. First she was afflicted with a kind of tunnel vision, and then with a foreshortening of her field of view. By mid-month she could see nothing that was more than about a foot away from her eyes, nor could she recognize her own hand in front of her face. She became increasingly infantile. Her only possible position now was the horizontal, especially since the head rolled about uncontrollably on her powerless neck when she was held upright. She emerged now more and more rarely. Finally, although it couldn't be clearly labeled as such, there was a last time.

Then it was Margaret's turn. She was already weakened by Sick Doris's deterioration and disappearance. Her tantrums, thus deprived of their principal object, became less frequent and less violent. The Princes embarked on a program of keeping her asleep and otherwise restricting her activities as much as they could without irritating her. As the months passed, signs of deterioration began to appear, but the process was much slower than it had been for the less energetic Sick Doris. It also took a somewhat different form; there was less lethargy involved, and the evidence of mental growth reversal was clearer. She seemed to speak and behave more like a nine-year-old, then an eight-, a seven-, a six-year-old and so on. By September, 1912, she began childishly compressing the pronunciation of words ("brekit" for "break-fast"), and two months later a German accent and German expressions appeared, presumably a reinstituted vestige of her acquaintance, at the age of five, with a group of German farmhands. The name Fischer no longer meant anything to her, and she had no recollection of her parents. Her vision was failing, as were her other senses (except, curiously, her sense of touch, which developed prodigiously).

In the meantime Doris, of course, was enjoying a great revival. When Margaret lost her sight entirely, for example, Doris reported an enormous improvement in *her* vision. But overall progress still was frustratingly slow. It was September, 1913, before Doris was managing to remain in control for as long as 24 hours at a time. In February, 1914, she stayed on top from the 22nd through most of the 25th, for a total of almost 71 hours. From hours and days these periods lengthened to weeks, and by May she had proved so thoroughly in command of herself—only Sleeping Margaret emerged occasionally, and that may have been all to the good—that Dr. Prince and his neurologist colleague tentatively but confidently declared her cured.

Patience Worth, 1919

In 1914, Mrs. John Curran of St. Louis was thirty years old. She had received no education beyond grammar school; had done only a little reading in her life, all of it quite light and casual; and had traveled very little in the United States, and none at all abroad. She had no experience whatsoever in any kind of writing, nor any perceptible talent for it. Yet in that year of 1914 she began writing professionally, and quite successfully, under the name of Patience Worth. This name, however, was no mere pen name. Patience Worth, a secondary personality, was a woman of wide, varied and extremely versatile writing talent. As for Mrs. Curran, her writing was what is called "automatic," dictated by her alter ego.

By 1919—the year in which her case was reported by Charles E. Cory in the *Psychological Review*—Patience had completed more than a thousand poems, a play or two, and a couple of novels (both published by Henry Holt & Co.). In addition, she was working on four more novels, moving from one to another with complete ease and faultless memory. The two published novels had received enthusiastic notices in journals of repute, including New York's *Sun*, *Times*, and *Mirror*, and Boston's *Transcript*. The reviews were studded with nouns like "beauty," "poetry," and "power," and with adjectives like "wonderful," "beautiful," and "noble."

Both of the published works were historical novels. *The Sorry Tale*, a long and complicated story of Roman and Jewish cultures at about the time of Christ, was a monument to the author's vast erudition. *Hope Trueblood* showed a similarly detailed knowledge of nineteenth-century England. These and her other works revealed great stores of special information and an astonishing variety of literary styles and approaches, difficult to associate with a single writer. Small wonder that Mrs. Curran and her husband considered Patience Worth as a spirit of genius, intermittently in possession of Mrs. Curran's body and worthy of the utmost reverence.

Such reverential awe on Mrs. Curran's part is certainly understandable. She was actively interested in spiritualism and had often attended seances. From her viewpoint Patience Worth was an unseen and irresistible power who could plunge her into a spell of unconsciousness at will. After these spells Mrs. Curran usually would find a large chunk of manuscript—as much as four or five thousand words might be written in two or three hours—which her husband and others had watched her write in the person of Patience Worth. Only occasionally would she have a dim recollection of her own role as transcriber.

The difference between the two personalities was more than merely unmistakeable. Mrs. Curran was by no means a clod; she was mentally alert, quick to understand. But her fund of knowledge was quite limited, and her interests did not go much beyond house and husband. Patience Worth was a brilliant, knowledgeable, versatile conversationalist whose talents in this respect quite matched the literary abilities that she continually demonstrated. Her breadth of knowledge, her fluency and even eloquence, her sophistication, her learning *au courant,* and so on—none of these characteristics could be explained in terms of Mrs. Curran's intelligence, education or concerns. It might have been easier, for example, to explain Portia the lawyer in terms of Mrs. Micawber, or Margaret Mead in terms of Edith Bunker.

Her literary work, Patience informed Dr. Corey, required a great deal of thought and planning so that the actual writing could be done very rapidly in the limited time available. Thus while Mrs. Curran busied herself each day with housework, Patience quite separately would be mapping out the next portion of a current novel. Mrs. Curran would be quite unaware of this, although Patience was quite conscious of Mrs. Curran's activities and even her thoughts. This Mary-and-Martha division of labor, thoroughly satisfactory to both parties, might well be the envy of most writers and artists. One could hardly find an arrangement more convenient for creative activity.

Both personalities exhibited complete rationality in word and deed. Mrs. Curran's dissociations can be considered instances of insanity only if one ignores the large complement of perfectly normal Worth-watchers. Patience Worth's conversation was consistently a model of rationality—with one exception. She vigorously and persuasively maintained that she was the disembodied spirit of an Englishwoman who had died many decades, if not centuries, before. Whether this was her idea or Mrs. Curran's never became clear, since an opportunity for psychoanalysis never presented itself.

After publishing his article in 1919, Dr. Cory evidently lost touch with Mrs. Curran, probably because of the pressures of his regular caseload. A promised follow-up article never appeared. As a result, Mrs. Curran and Patience Worth faded together into the mists of unrecorded history.

Alice, 1919

If Alice had been Spanish, there might never have been any need for Bonita. But Alice wasn't Spanish.

In her teens (at about the turn of the century) she attended a convent school where three of the students, all from Mexico, spoke Spanish a great deal in her presence. This inclusion-exclusion experience doubtless was a very trying one, although she did not particularly complain about it. In any case, it seems to have laid the groundwork for the fluent pseudo-Spanish to be displayed later.

Her convent schooling ended abruptly with a deeply traumatic event, when her father committed suicide at the age of 56, leaving the mother to cope with their six children. In his report on this case in 1919 ("A Divided Self," in the *Journal of Abnormal Psychology*), Charles E. Cory described the mother's role laconically and rather cryptically: "The mother's side is negative." But a picture of a mother-dominated household, with a browbeaten father seeking refuge in heavy drinking and ultimately in total withdrawal, is not hard to conjure up. For Alice, at least, the father evidently was a haven of understanding and affection.

His death clearly was a staggering blow. Alice suffered a temporary loss of coordination; as she described it, she later had to learn how to walk all over again. She became moody, unpredictable. Occasionally she seemed to lose control of herself, as on those nights when she would rise from her bed and dance about her room with spirited abandon. Her condition continued to deteriorate, though slowly, over the next several years. Then one evening in 1916, when she was 26, she heard someone singing. As she moved about the room, trying to locate the source of the singing, she became aware that the sound didn't change in volume or direction with her movements, and indeed that it was coming from inside herself. When it stopped for a moment, she asked, silently, who it was that was singing. The answer came from within her, but unmistakably. This was the first time that she heard the name Bonita. And Bonita, it turned out, was Spanish.

78

Shortly after her father's death, Alice had met and had become thoroughly infatuated with an older man who looked Spanish, spoke Spanish, and boasted a Spanish mother. This affair occurred during Bonita's gradual development into a secondary personality, and its influence on her was incalculable. By the time that Alice and Bonita hove into view on Dr. Cory's horizon, they were ostensibly two quite different people inhabiting the same body. Alice was quiet, reserved, diffident, easily fatigued. Her health generally was good enough for her to perform well in her job as sales clerk, but she often came home from work too tired to do anything but collapse for the evening. Bonita, in contrast, was downright bouncy, chock-full of both energy and self-assurance. When Alice came home too exhausted even to eat, Bonita often would emerge, gobble up her supper, and have a thoroughly enjoyable evening for herself. Her respiration, Dr. Cory discovered during a couple of physical examinations, was both deeper and more rapid than Alice's, her eyes were brighter, her skin more glowing. In a sense she seemed to be the *joie de vivre* that had eluded Alice, personified.

To Dr. Cory's surprise, Bonita proved quite knowledgeable, even sophisticated, about Alice's condition. Although Alice seemed the more cultured and better educated of the two, she had not learned much beyond the elementary fact that Bonita was a dissociated personality; when this realization helped clear up most of the mysteries of her troubled past, she seemed satisfied, not wishing to delve any further. It was Bonita who had read Morton Prince's works on the unconscious and on the Christine Beauchamp case, as well as a number of other books on abnormal psychology. She did not find them difficult reading, she absorbed the information readily, and she discussed the subject with the doctor lucidly and articulately. But all this brilliant display, it turned out, was quite detached and academic. Bonita could not bring herself to apply her considerable knowledge and understanding to her own case.

When she had first appeared, Bonita had told Alice that she, Bonita, was the long-departed spirit of a Spanish woman. (Alice had become quite the cynosure in a group of spiritualistic friends.) Bonita never abandoned this notion. She immersed herself in things Spanish, or sometimes in things that she merely fancied were Spanish. Food with a Spanish flavor, clothes with a Spanish flair, dancing in the flamenco style—anything and everything Spanish was invariably to her taste. She spoke English with a strong Spanish accent. Her Spanish, rapid and mellifluous, doubtless sounded quite genuine to someone not acquainted with the language. Actually, however, it was an untranslatable mishmash of Spanish, and Spanish-sounding, words and phrases. She was quite astonished, and doubtless very chagrined, when Dr. Cory demonstrated to her that she herself couldn't translate a transcription of her chatter into intelligible English.

Even this revelation did nothing to shake her firm delusion. Her former self, she was convinced, had been a strapping woman, physically strong, sexually excitable and exciting, and passionate to the fullest extent of the Latin tradition. She had only contempt for Alice's fragility and reserve. Under hypnosis she considered herself the most irresistible of sirens, having left in her wake a long train of spent lovers. In Alice's body she felt hopelessly caged.

What finally happened to Alice and Bonita we do not know. As in the case of Mrs. Curran and Patience Worth, Dr. Cory published his report during the period of dissociations but evidently was unable to report later as to the outcome. His articles are rather academic in tone and approach, and he may have been much more interested in observation than in therapy. This would be understandable in view of how little was known about ways to heal this mental and emotional disease—even less than now.

Violet, 1922

Violet had an extraordinary talent for being a medium. But since she apparently lacked the necessary faith, she never became a full-fledged medium. Yet her automatic writing was spectacular enough to be brought to the attention of psychiatrists in New England, where she lived, shortly before the first World War and to be reported, in 1922 by Dr. Anita Muhl, in the *Journal of Abnormal Psychology.*

Violet's early years were quite ordinary, except in the sense that her family's affluence gave her more than ordinary advantages, including attendance at a good finishing school and a college for women. Her health, including her mental health, was splendid. She suffered from no nervous disorders, showed no hysterical tendencies. She had studied psychology in college, although her major in English had not allowed her enough time to take elective courses in abnormal psychology. Sociology had been one of her main interests in school, and she had put her training to work in social service activities in Boston for a while after graduation. Her primary interest, however, seems to have been in English. Not only did she take up the teaching of that subject, but in addition she married a college professor of English in a western city. Intelligent and charming, she apparently adjusted quite well to the academic life.

As time passed, however, her schedule became burdensome, including as it did her own teaching, her household duties, and the social demands of a rather inbred community. Her periods of fatigue became more and more frequent, until finally she consulted the family doctor. He perceptively diagnosed her problem as being one of fatigue, perhaps slightly complicated by a minor heart irregularity. This visit proved to be only the first of many, not only with this doctor but with some others, including some psychologists and psychiatrists.

For better or worse, Violet had developed an interest in the ouija board in recent years, and now, she told the doctor, she had found that the board worked better than ever for her during her periods of fatigue.

This interested him, perhaps because it suggested a possible therapy. At the next opportunity, he decided, he would explore her aptitude for automatic writing in a state of fatigue. (Automatic writing was generally considered a step up from the ouija board.) If her persistent fatigue was psychosomatic, the automatic writing might provide an outlet for whatever she might be repressing, a release of the tensions which might be draining her energy.

After a few false starts, Violet quickly got the hang of it, and soon her automatic writing was a wonder to behold. Her hand flew across the page, filling sheet after sheet, as a growing case of personalities emerged and dictated—or wrote out—their views on a multitude of subjects. Each introduced himself or herself by name, and each could be identified by a distinctive style of handwriting. They would appear singly or in groups of as many as five or six, and in the latter event they could be quite unruly and impolite to one another. Some were minor and very indistinct, appearing too rarely to reveal much about their characters; others were major, perfectly distinct, and (some of them) all too fond of visiting. Once identified, they usually would come when called by name—"Yes, this is Annie," Violet's hand might write, "what is it you want?" As for Violet herself, sometimes she knew what her hand was writing, sometimes not. Although she conducted herself differently with the emergence of the different personalities, she generally seemed to maintain her own character until, after about three months of this experimenting, her doctor and his fascinated colleagues became concerned over how close she seemed to be to dissociating, and called a halt to the whole affair.

The earliest, most frequent, and most garrulous visitor called herself Annie McGinnis. Although Violet had never been able to draw anything much more complicated than a straight line, Annie drew a cunning self-portrait to distinguish herself from the other personalities, including Violet. Hers was a story to be told over the wailing of violins. Born and reared in poverty, she had been cozened by a man with a smooth tongue and a specious offer to take her away from all that. After a spell of service in a brothel, she had become pregnant and had died in childbirth. A period of suffering and spiritual vagrancy followed, and then she had come across the virtuous Violet, in whose company she found great comfort. And so, figuratively speaking, she had moved in and settled down.

"Settled" perhaps is not the word for use in connection with Annie, who was as full of restless energy as Violet was enervated. Her handwriting was rough and rapid; she never had enough time and always had plenty to say. She was irascible and rudely impatient, wild and full of sudden passions. And, like Somerset Maugham's celebrated tart, Miss Thompson, she hated men. Oh, how she hated men! Sometimes, in her anger and frustration, she would stamp her feet on the floor and slam her fists on the table, to Violet's considerable pain and dismay. Indeed, writing for Annie was never a pleasant experience for Violet, who almost always lived through it with body rigid, lips set, teeth clenched, and eyes wide with apprehension and even fright.

She was much more comfortable with Mary Patterson, who of all the secondary personalities most closely resembled Violet in her handwriting, use of English, and general behavior. Unfortunately, she appeared only rarely, since she was not aggressive enough to compete successfully with the more boisterous personalities, who were persistently demanding the floor and who rudely expropriated it from her on the few occasions when she did have it.

Mary Minott, another major personality, was an urbane, svelte, sophisticated city girl who considered Mary Patterson a weak-kneed, puritanical prissy. She was very impatient with Violet, whom she offered to introduce to the world of dress designing, where fame and fortune awaited her. To prove her point she designed a number of dresses, exhibiting what the doctors considered downright genius. It need hardly be added that Violet, on her own, could no more design a dress than she could build a cantilever bridge. And perhaps that's why she never did accept Mary Minott's pressing invitation.

Her deceased father was another of the personalities who appeared only seldom. This was not because he was diffident like Mary Patterson, but apparently because he was busy. When he did appear, Dr. Muhl reported, he "only made hurried remarks about family affairs" and disappeared like the harried rabbit in *Alice in Wonderland*. The handwriting that resulted from these brief visits was compared with samples of the dead father's handwriting; it was the same.

Two of the personalities constantly urged Violet to become a medium, thus putting her enormous talent to its full use. One of these was Alton, who was very unusual in that there was a real, live Alton who was a friend of Violet's fiance. She didn't like him in the flesh, and this more mystical version wasn't any more attractive. In this latter form she wasn't quite sure what he was up to, for he addressed her in very affectionate terms, apparently trying to get her to break her engagement and to play Héloise to his Abelard. He was much more direct in his efforts to persuade her to graduate from automatic writing to the status of medium. There were hazards involved, he conceded, but he was confident that he could protect her from them. She was not so confident.

The other personality who was interested in her becoming a medium called himself the "Spirit of War and Desolation." The United States was to enter the war shortly, and the Spirit regaled Violet and the doctors in attendance with harrowing depictions of the Armageddon to come. In addition to becoming a medium, he advised Violet, she should join the Red Cross.

The last of the personalities to appear was the one who so alarmed the doctors that they abruptly called the whole thing off. Like the Spirit, he preferred a measure of anonymity, identifying himself simply as "Man." At first his character was quite vague, quite blurred and shadowy, like the dim figure of a man half hidden in a heavy fog. Gradually he became more distinct, alternating with Alton in his appearances. This alternating arrangement seems not to have worked out very well for Alton, who became the object of the Man's intense hostility and soon was replaced by him altogether.

As the Man grew stronger, the other personalities grew weaker, with one conspicuous exception, Annie. Their relationship was pure and simple: unadulterated mutual hatred—on Annie's part expressed in two-inch lettering. The Man tried to get rid of her, but she was as strong as he. She took great joy in defacing the written record of his comments with aimless scribbling. Perhaps this was her eventual undoing, for it angered him intensely and he seemed to draw strength from this anger. For some time there were only the two of them, setting poor Violet's nerves on edge with their quarreling. But then there was only one.

Now alone with Violet, the Man not only continued to grow stronger but also became bolder. He seemed to infuse her with some of his energy, so that under his influence she often felt a strong desire to do something physically active. As if in response, he began urging her to dance. With every such invitation she grew more and more tempted, but in each instance her ennui and her Puritan heritage won out. Each time, however, she seemed stronger and that heritage seemed weaker, and finally one day, when the Man was being particularly insistent, she rose from her writing table and began dancing around the room, slowly at first and then faster and more violently. Fortunately the dance was a brief one, ending suddenly when, after lurching forward and uttering a piercing scream, she fell exhausted to the floor. Placed on a couch, she lay there for some ten minutes, her body rigid, her throat vibrant with a low, incessant moan.

When she finally relaxed enough to discuss the experience, she described it as a frightening one, chiefly because she had felt that she was losing control of her body to someone else. This suggestion of dissociation in turn frightened the doctors, who advised her to give up all automatic writing forthwith. She found, however, that she couldn't break the habit all that suddenly; she did have some contact with the Man a few times thereafter, but the visits were brief and much calmer. Soon after this she was married, and automatic writing activities were superseded for several months. Then one day, happening to be alone and idle, she tried it again, but the Man did not respond. Instead, Mary Patterson appeared and solemnly informed Violet that all the other personalities, including the Man, were now too weak to emerge, and indeed she was feeling rather poorly herself. This was Violet's last attempt to call out any of them.

Throughout the experiment she had shown a highly intelligent interest in the proceedings. She tried valiantly to discern, through assiduous introspection, the origin of each of the personalities. Annie, for instance, may have arisen out of the guilt Violet dimly felt when her social work had brought her into contact with other women who had not been as fortunate as she—"There, but for the grace of God, go I." Annie's opinion of men, Violet thought, may have been simply the unconscious reverse of Violet's own conscious attitude. Similarly the Man, with his aggressive energy and his inclination to dominate, may have brought to the surface some suppressed tendencies that Violet could never consciously acknowledge. One of the personalities had thoroughly puzzled her: Alton, who was a living, external personality. Then she remembered a discussion with her mother shortly after she had met the real Alton, a discussion that she felt explained his appearance and his enticing conversation. Shortly after this revelation, Alton disappeared forever.

Her understanding of her condition may not have been entirely accurate, but no one else was in a position to offer anything better. Apparently it constituted adequate therapy. Violet was comfortably married now and, at least so far as dissociations were concerned, she presumably lived happily ever after.

Mabel, 1931

In September, 1915, Mabel, age 25, was admitted to London's Devon Mental Hospital, where her father had died of "general paralysis" more than twenty years earlier. She had swallowed a package of pins and had been medically certified as subject to depression and suicidal impulses. She had something of a reputation for strange behavior. Some sixteen months earlier she had been sued in court for writing libelous letters about herself and then accusing someone else of writing them. During her eleven months at Devon she often talked about suicide and sometimes wounded herself slightly, apparently in an effort to provide at least some tentative evidence of her serious intent. Although she gained weight in the hospital, she was a dedicated hypochondriac, continually coming up with inexplicable aches and pains which of course required immediate attention.

In August, 1916, she was transferred to another hospital, where examination under hypnosis revealed a coterie of more than half a dozen personalities alternately inhabiting her body. Mabel herself seemed to be the primary personality, although she was neurotic and incorrigibly unhappy. In contrast, Biddy was cheerful, genial, lighthearted, and considerate of others. Another personality, nameless, seemed to appear when the patient's face assumed a look of malice. Hope, Faith and Dame Trot appeared too seldom to take on clearly distinct characters. The same seemed to be true of Miss Take, who also was nameless but who described herself as "just a mistake." The most important of the secondary personalities, however, was Miss Dignity— Mabel's father had taken to calling her "Little Miss Dignity" before he died—and she was really the only one who kept the whole affair from seeming like nothing more than a good-natured put-on. Indeed, her reason for being evidently was to make life as uncomfortable for Mabel as possible.

To this end, without Mabel's direct knowledge—none of the personalities knew what any of the others did—Miss Dignity regularly

86

wreaked havoc in Mabel's life by destroying her clothes, discarding her jewelry, shredding her paper money. Sometimes she did such things simply out of malice, but more often the malice was triggered by irritation at not being called out for a long time. On one occasion Mabel found so little of her underclothing left in one piece that she couldn't keep warm. On another, she had so little unshredded money left that she had to live on small portions of bread and tea for several days. She had come to the unsettling conclusion that such things were being done to her by some other personality within herself. During this period she suffered from bad health, including hysterical loss of voice and some paralysis of the legs. Her condition was not improved by frequent discoveries of unpleasant letters addressed to her in varied handwriting, including a note from Miss Dignity recommending suicide, with poison thoughtfully enclosed. Some of the handwriting (not Miss Dignity's) was badly formed, like a child's, suggesting that the personalities were of different ages.

In 1927, Mabel was referred to Dr. Robert Riggall, a psychoanalyst and clinical psychologist at the West End Hospital for Nervous Disorders. This account of the case comes from his brief report in *The Lancet* for October 17, 1931. By the time of the referral all of Mabel's secondary personalities had disappeared except Miss Dignity, who was still pursuing her vigorous policy of harassment.

The doctor saw his patient in 28 interviews over a period of six months. Most of the time she would arrive at his office as Mabel, but for five of the interviews she arrived as Miss Dignity. In either case, the other personality would emerge under hypnosis, invariably impressing the doctor with the marked differences in "speech, expression, and whole demeanor," as well as personality. Mabel, he discovered, was a devout, idealistic Roman Catholic, very conscious of the strictures of her faith. She was unusually narcissistic, with a persistent need for sympathetic consideration of her maltreatment by Miss Dignity. And, as might be expected, she was a model of feminine propriety.

Miss Dignity was quite her opposite. Beyond her resentment at being repressed by Mabel, she was in rebellion against the inhibitions imposed by society and especially by Mabel's religious principles. If she could be called devoted to anything, it was to pleasure, including sexual pleasure. Since her opportunities in this respect were of course severely limited, she evidently was willing to take rather unconventional measures in attempts to satisfy her needs. During one interview, for example, Mabel told the doctor that she was experiencing sharp pains in the groin area when she walked or sat down. The doctor, after putting her into a hypnotic trance, called out Miss Dignity and asked if she could offer any explanation. Her response more than justified his suspicions. Before the interview, at home, she had placed a broken wineglass in Mabel's (and her own) vagina. Why? To irritate Mabel, of course, in more ways than one. But why her vagina? So that she, Miss Dignity, would be able to enjoy some erotic sensations when the doctor removed the intruder, as he promptly did (and as, presumably, she did). Fortunately Mabel knew nothing of any of this, beyond the pain and discomfort, or she might have died of mortification.

By the 28th session the doctor had managed, through hypnotic suggestion, to fuse the two personalities together solidly enough for him to feel that Miss Dignity was gone for good. He was by no means satisfied, however, that he had cured Mabel; he felt rather that he had simply, and rather artificially, shifted her neurosis to the single personality. To get at the neurosis, he urged Mabel to undergo analysis, but in vain. And his misgivings were confirmed during a series of court cases in which he was called as a witness in her defense.

John Charles Poultney, 1933

Probably no collection of multiple-personality case histories should omit the case of John Charles Poultney, since it was the subject of one of the three single-case books published in this century, Shepherd Franz's *Persons, One and Three* (McGraw-Hill, 1933). Unfortunately, however, it is one of the least clear-cut cases on record because the book differentiates between the two personalities not on the basis of traits but rather from the chronological record that Dr. Franz had assiduously compiled on his patient's alternating periods of amnesia. (The third personality, if there was one, was always inchoate, created by inference to fill in unexplained gaps.)

This lack of character distinction may have been due to the nature of the case, for John Poultney's words and deeds, as reported, were not so very different from Charles Poulting's. The two of them spoke the same English, wrote the same hand, had the same gait, were impelled by the same work ethic, and so on. Each remembered things from the other's life, often without knowing it, in a kind of confused blending that distinguishes this case probably more than any other feature.

Yet the man's life could hardly be described as that of a well-integrated personality. The real John Poultney first stood up in Ireland, where he was born in 1888. He went through the usual procedure: school, work, marriage, children (two sons). In 1905 he joined the army, served his hitch with the regulars, and was put on reserve in 1907, the year he was married. He learned to drive several different makes of automobile (they were much different from one another in those early, experimental days) and earned a modest living as a chauffeur and truck driver. In 1913, apparently unable to find a steady job, he sailed for the United States to seek his fortune. Not finding it in New York, he traveled about (Detroit, Cleveland, Chicago, Toledo), reconciling himself to $15-a-week jobs with Studebaker and Sears, Roebuck. When Great Britain declared war on Germany in 1914, he returned to Dublin and his reserve outfit, was assigned to a transport unit, and was shipped to a garrison outside London, there to await transportation to France. While waiting, he was promoted to sergeant. It was now September, 1914, and he was destined never to remember anything that happened during the next five or six months.

In February or March of 1915, a very confused man found himself convalescing in a London hospital. He had no conscious memory of anything that had happened in his life up to that moment. He was told that his name was C.J. Poulting; this may have been because of unclear writing on his admission card, but he was so unsure of himself that he accepted the name and kept it. He had been brought back from Belgium with a head wound, one of a group of Belgian refugees. His uniform and any identification cards or papers that he may have carried had disappeared. Indeed, at first he had been classified as a Belgian, but the authorities later decided, after a physical examination, that he must be an American because of the tattoos of Buffalo Bill and the American flag on his arms (both were mementos from Poultney's visit to Toledo). Poulting, after a few weeks of this uncertainty and distress, was highly vulnerable to a recruiting sergeant's suggestion that the army would be glad to establish an identity for him if he'd care to join up. Since by then he was in satisfactory health physically, he did join up, officially becoming C.J. Poulting of Florida, U.S.A., Private No. M2/967530.

An instance of the unconscious linkage between the two personalities occurred when the time came for him to be given a permanent assignment. One morning the recruits were lined up and asked a series of questions about their qualifications and previous work experience. At one point those with driving experience were asked to step forward, and Poulting did so at once without thinking. Later that day he was taken to a field crowded with cars of all varieties, where he quickly demonstrated his competence in handling a standard American model. Curiously, the non-American cars were strange to him, and he had to learn to drive them, although the driving that he had done in Ireland was much more extensive than the little bit of test driving that he had done for Studebaker.

And so he became a driver in the British army, seeing plenty of action throughout northern France, in Flanders, and at Ypres, where he was gassed and returned to England as a casualty. In December, 1915, having recovered enough for reassignment, he was shipped to Africa. On the way there, after violating blackout security by lighting a cigarette at night, he was clapped in the brig, where he was given a long-term sample of that fine old naval tradition of hanging men up by their thumbs. The trip apparently had been very uncomfortable for him anyway, since he was having trouble with brief dissociations. (The dim third personality may have been in operation here, since neither Poultney nor Poulting could later recall anything that had occurred during such blackouts.) In addition, conditions in the brig were intolerable. One morning a guard found him hanging by a hammock rope from a beam in his cell and cut him down in the nick of time. The ship's officers released him from his confinement with the understanding that he would not report his mistreatment.

During 1916 he saw a great deal of action in Africa as an ambulance driver, had several memory lapses, contracted a severe case of malaria, and was returned to England to recuperate. While in Africa he had two experiences with leopards, at least one of which later proved significant. The first occurred after he and a buddy had been captured and had escaped, making their way cross-country alone in a direction which they hoped would lead them to the nearest British troops. At night they slept in the open. Each evening Poulting would climb into a tree and tie himself to a branch, feeling that this might offer some protection against any hungry wild animals—especially leopards, which were prevalent in the area—but his buddy, considering it not worth the effort, slept on the ground. One moonless, pitchblack night Poulting was awakened by sounds of struggle, mixed with deep growling and muffled cries, and the next morning he could see what little remained. The leopards, no longer hungry, had disappeared. He went blank, and the next thing he knew he was in a hospital in Nairobi, awaiting transfer to a convalescent hospital in Voi, about 250 miles away.

On the way to Voi he picked up a small monkey and adopted it as a pet. He became very fond of it, keeping it on a leash in his hut. Its chattering sometimes proved annoying, however, and one night he tethered it outside, a few yards away from the hut. In the middle of the night he heard it cry out and, in the moonlight, watched helplessly as a leopard tore it from its leash and carried it off. This second incident was much more traumatic for him than the first, since his personal responsibility for the animal's death resulted in deep feelings of guilt. But the trauma was to prove a blessing about a dozen years later.

Early in 1917, he was shipped back to England with malaria. After a few weeks in the hospital he was sent across the Channel again, this time to work with ammunition supply columns in France and Belgium. Injured in an explosion in Belgium, he was brought back to a hospital in Woolwich, where he was given a medical discharge and a small pension. After a spell of futile job-hunting, he joined the Red Cross as a driver. In Calais, during an air raid, he was injured again, this time while rescuing patients from the flaming ruins of a hospital, in an exhibition of heroism for which he received the Croix de Guerre. After his recovery in England, he visited his family in Dublin, although neither Poulting nor Poultney ever had any memory of the visit whatsoever. In April, 1918, the British military "returned" him to the United States, where he spent the rest of the war as a Liberty Bond speaker at rallies held by the Red Cross, the Knights of Columbus, and the YMCA. He was, after all, a war hero.

The months after the Armistice saw a rapid devaluation of war medals. He took off on a job hunt that carried him as far west as he could go, and in 1920 he wound up in Los Angeles, washing and greasing automobiles. He did this work in that burgeoning town for about the next ten years with varying degrees of success, ranging from owning his own business to being unemployed. His biggest problem, he said later, was that as soon as he had accumulated some money he would get a yen to travel and would forsake everything to go on a trip. Although he didn't remember them all later, he made three trips to Florida, four to Panama, and at least one to New York and to Cuba, among others. On his fourth trip to Panama he was in a blackout from a day or so before he decided to go until he arrived at the Canal, just as the passengers were leaving the ship. He was surprised to find himself there but was happy to hear that he had been the life of the party during the voyage. The ship's officers, who had been aware of the presence of an extra passenger but also had been reluctant to conduct an extensive identity check, were sympathetic about his amnesia and arranged with the port authorities for his return to Los Angeles on the next ship going that way. (This may have been his only return trip that did not include a hassle with the immigration officials.) And thus, in sum, did he spend The Roaring Twenties living and working in Los Angeles, more or less.

On a December morning in 1929, he was picked up by the police in Los Angeles as he was wandering aimlessly and rather unsteadily down a deserted street. Reversing the usual procedure, he asked them what his name was, and then what date this was. They were able to identify him by some newspaper clippings and the discharge papers he was carrying. As his confusion gradually cleared, he began acting more normally but, as Charles Poulting, still could not give them any biographical details earlier than 1915. Somehow the American Legion became interested in his predicament (doubtless some of the police officers were members) and asked Dr. Franz, who was in the Department of Psychology at the University of California at Los Angeles, to interview him in an attempt to extract further information that might help to identify him.

Soon the newspapers got into the act, and as a result of the publicity he was besieged not only by the idly curious but also by people eager to welcome him back as a long-lost father, son or brother. The most persistent of this latter group were a Mrs. Herrman and her daughter Mrs. Dandy, who took him to the home that they shared, firmly convinced that he *must* be Charles Stuart Herrman, who had left home in 1913 and had not been heard from since 1914. Whether young Herrman had found the two ladies hard to live with is not recorded (Dr. Franz's chief informant here was Mrs. Dandy), but Poulting certainly did, partly because of their stifling solicitude and partly because of the rigors of their Seventh-Day Adventism. And so in mid-February, 1930, *he* left home. Six days later the San Francisco police found him wandering about in a dazed condition, and he was returned to his home and his loved ones. (He now carried cards in his wallet with the names of a Los Angeles police official, a Hollywood doctor, and Dr. Franz.) But after a week or so he again left home, this time for good, and moved into a friend's apartment.

He also discontinued his daily visits to Dr. Franz, who had been accumulating a good deal of information on the 1915-30 portion of his life but nothing on his earlier years. On March 4, the Los Angeles police phoned the doctor to tell him that they had found Poulting again wandering about the streets in a daze. He didn't know who he was or where he was, and he resolutely refused to accept the ridiculous suggestion that he could be in Los Angeles, California. After he had been brought to Dr. Franz's office, he mumbled complaints about the police driving on the wrong side of the street; he asked what had happened to his uniform and made vague references to an imminent departure with his regiment. He recognized neither Dr. Franz nor his friend the police official. Eagerly, Dr. Franz asked him to write his name on a piece of paper, and he wrote "19463 Sgt. John Charles J. Poultney." And then he crossed out the "J." Poultney was back, but evidently Poulting still had a toehold.

Poultney had to be shown several recent newspapers and his own aging visage in a mirror before he would begin to believe that he was indeed in California in the year 1930. As he warmed up to the gently solicitous Dr. Franz, he began to talk quite freely. The interview that followed was an exciting one for Dr. Franz, as he learned all the details about the other half of his patient. Poultney remembered his life up to 1915 clearly, but nothing thereafter. In an effort to help merge the two memory sets while Poultney was still susceptible to suggestion, toward the end of the interview the doctor showed his patient a large map of Africa and asked if he recognized any of the place names. The ex-sergeant pored over the map, looking at names that had been familiar to Poulting with great interest but no sign of recognition until he came across the town of Voi. "Voi!" he cried excitedly. "I was there—I had a monkey!" That seemed to break the dam. Poulting's memories flooded his mind too rapidly for him to describe them. Dr. Franz, almost in alarm, closed the interview and told his patient to get some rest, at least as best he could under the circumstances.

The next day Poultney was given a brief autobiography that Poulting had written on the occasion of his first interview. Poultney was fascinated, of course, by this confirmation of his new memories, and the experience furthered the process of integration. During the next twelve months the process continued, with only occasional relapses. (When he went to see the movie, *All Quiet on the Western Front*, for instance, he shouted in panic during a battle scene and "took cover" in the orchestra pit. Thereafter he avoided war movies.)

Meanwhile, Dr. Franz dispatched discreet inquiries to his patient's relatives in Ireland. This started a correspondence, especially with the wife, that eventually convinced Poultney that he should rejoin his family. He did so in July, 1931. The last thing Dr. Franz heard from him was a thank-you note in which he seemed to have become a reasonably contented and well-integrated single personality. At least this was true by contrast, and in the contrast at least there was hope.

Harriet, 1933

Harriet was born in 1902, near the end of her mother's seventh month of pregnancy. During her first year she was a crybaby in spades, a squalling infant who gave her parents little peace and much cause for anxiety. As she grew older she exhibited an extraordinary degree of restlessness, which among other things took the form of several determined, if thwarted, attempts to leave home. In 1911, at the age of nine, she began showing signs of hysteria: brief fainting spells, at first months and later weeks apart, in which she alternated between laughing and crying and would (her mother reported) "shake all over in coming out of them." Sometimes an arm would hurt; at other times a leg would grow stiff. Once she was paralyzed below the waist for two months, without any feeling in her legs.

Her childhood was generally pretty unpleasant. Her behavior toward her elders and peers was predominantly dyspeptic, with plenty of quarreling and resentments among all concerned. Her father punished her often and severely for her continual failures to help her mother with the household work, although his stern justice often was frustrated by the advent of one of her fainting spells. These failures to help her mother, as well as more positive instances of misbehavior, were generally among the things that she didn't remember later. Indeed, much of the quarreling arose from her contention that people were continually lying about her, accusing her of doing bad things that she was sure she hadn't done. It didn't occur to anyone that she might be having spells of genuine amnesia, especially since she had a reputation for fancifully embroidering the truth on other occasions and in other respects.

As she approached her teens she became obsessively fond of movies and romantic novels. Her memory, whatever its lapses, proved highly accurate and detailed with regard to her favorite love scenes and passages. Her identification with some of the heroines, or variants thereof, became quite firmly fixed in her imagination. Sometimes she described herself as a Chicago showgirl who could tap dance (as indeed she did, though without a lesson), sometimes as a society girl whom a rejected suitor had enrolled in a brothel, sometimes as a New York wife embroiled in an all-consuming affair of uncontrollable passion, and so on.

She began working for wages at fourteen, an age that was not considered so tender sixty years ago. Despite some trouble in holding jobs, she did manage to augment the family income over the next several years. Perhaps the loss of this supplement, however unreliable, weighed on her parents' minds when she began showing more than ordinary interest in a young man named George. In any case, when she announced her intention of marrying him they objected so strenuously and repeatedly that on one occasion she ended a quarrel by going into a trance and remaining in it for two solid days. Her parents punched her, shook her, pinched her, tossed water in her face, but she barely emerged from unconsciousness only two or three times, and then only to assure an imaginary George, wistfully, that her mother really did love him. Her father continued in his stern, unyielding opposition, and she continued having spells until finally the wedding took place over all objections. Such can be the fruits of parental prohibitions.

Harriet's marriage was no less full of turmoil, especially after the first baby was born. She began behaving more erratically than ever, George later reported. Most evenings, when he arrived home from work, she would be a glowing picture of domestic responsibility, with the house neat, supper ready, the child well cared for. Sometimes, however, he would be greeted by an empty house, a deserted kitchen, and an abandoned, squalling baby. On these occasions, he soon learned from a variety of sources, his wife would be out walking the streets, idly window-shopping, and "carrying on" with *ad hoc* male acquaintances. After she was found and brought home, by George or by others, he would give her a severe tongue-lashing. During his lecture, or shortly thereafter, she would lapse momentarily into a trance and then emerge from it as the sober, responsible Harriet whose conduct as wife and mother he so admired. Nevertheless, she continued to irritate him by denying any recollection of the events of the preceding several hours—even, on one occasion, when brought face to face with a man she had been flirting with less than an hour before.

With each such incident George grew angrier at what he considered her stubborn lying, as well as her disreputable behavior. Unfortunately, he finally decided that a few sound beatings would knock some sense into her. Instead, of course, under the new policy her dissociations grew more frequent and more intense. The hoydenish secondary personality grew ever more vivid, more real, and if anything more irresponsible. She now had a name, "Susie." As a result of Susie's burgeoning and busy schedule, the baby died of neglect. Harriet was heartbroken, but not Susie.

So George and Harriet had another baby. But this time it wasn't Harriet who actually gave birth; it was Susie, and she did it without anesthetic. Harriet, who continually complained of aches and pains and who was inordinately sensitive to experimental pinpricks, had required a general anesthetic for the birth of the first child, but Susie, who knew neither ache nor pain and who was quite insensible to pinpricks, bore the second child without pain or anesthetic.

The child survived. Shortly after the birth, a couple who lived nearby took the troubled family in. Mr. and Mrs. Fitch knew of Harriet's problem. Being of the diabolism school of Roman Catholicism, they considered Harriet intermittently possessed by devils, whom they hoped to exorcise. (Harriet later became a Catholic, to her mother's intense irritation but for her own peace of mind.) Their method seems to have been quite simple, involving impromptu incantations, novenas, vigil lights, and the lavish use of holy water. The latter seems to have been effective at times in ending a trance or spell; doubtless the water was relatively cool. But probably of greatest importance was the Fitches' attitude toward Harriet. Unlike her father and to some extent her husband, they did not blame her, did not upbraid her, did not try to make her feel inferior or guilty. They treated her not as a perpetrator of evil but as a victim of the devils that possessed her. As a result of this attitude, she had much less need to seek refuge in Susie.

For some time she had been under the intermittent care of a psychiatrist, Dr. Cornelius Wholey, who reported her case in the *American Journal of Psychiatry* in January, 1933. As part of his observations he took motion pictures of Harriet disappearing into and emerging from various personalities. Besides Harriet herself, he could distinguish at least three personalities: Susie, the most fully developed and carefree; Jack, a very male personality whose outstanding characteristic seems to have been intense disgust at being in a woman's body and in women's clothes (which he tended to shed); and The Baby, who behaved like a one-year-old, as in learning to walk by imitation. Their various types of behavior were quite evident and distinguishable in the movies, which the doctor showed at an annual meeting of the American Psychiatric Association in June, 1932. (None of these personalities, nor any of the others reported by the Fitches, would talk; what communication existed was conducted in writing.)

The movies of Harriet as The Baby were taken shortly after she had undergone an acutely traumatic experience. A priest of the Fitches' parish church had been very kind, patient, and understanding with her, much more of a father to her than her natural father had ever been. One Sunday morning as she was sitting in church with Mr. and Mrs. Fitch, a man in the pew in front of them turned around to ask if they had heard the news, that the priest had died the night before. "My God!" Harriet exclaimed, and then she fell in a dead faint. After a few minutes she was revived, more or less, but complained of feeling very sick. She was helped out to the car, and the Fitches drove her home. They spoke several times to Harriet in an effort to comfort her but received not a word in reply.

At home she was totally unresponsive, even catatonic. They put her into a chair, and she simply sat in it, staring into space without expression, until Susie unexpectedly emerged, not at the Fitches' behest but on her own initiative. Usually the carefree, happy personality, Susie now was showing signs of anxiety and confusion, as well as an unprecedented solicitude. There was something wrong with Harriet's brain, she reported, adding that her own thought processes didn't seem to be working very well either. The brain seemed to be asleep, as a foot or hand may "go to sleep" after circulation is cut off.

The Fitches didn't know what to do about that, but they had enough presence of mind to persuade Susie to take some food, since they feared that Harriet might be impossible to feed in her present state. After eating, Susie receded and Harriet emerged, still rigidly comatose but dreamily repeating the dead priest's name over and over. In the hope of shocking her out of this alarming condition, the Fitches flashed a photograph of the priest in front of her, to no avail. Other efforts—loud talking, playing music, and performing the more customary cabalistic functions—proved equally futile.

After a few days of this—with Harriet's near catatonia interrupted only when the Fitches called Susie out for meals—Mrs. Fitch, casting about desperately for ideas, thought of the trunk containing the first baby's clothes and general miscellany. She brought it to Harriet and opened it up before her. The effect was immediate and remarkable. Harriet suddenly came to life, reaching into the trunk and tenderly fondling the baby clothes, for all the world like an affectionate mother. Then gradually her demeanor changed subtly from that of mother to that of child (Dr. Wholey happened to be visiting, and he observed this himself), until eventually she was handling the trunk's contents with anything but tenderness. She spent the rest of the evening gaily throwing toys about the room, trying to disembowel a doll, and generally conducting herself like the year-old baby she had manifestly become. At bedtime she refused flatly to go to sleep. The weary Fitches called out the cooperative Susie, who did go to sleep for them—but it was The Baby who woke up in the morning.

She spent the next day mostly eating candy and ice cream. Like a baby, she tossed one ice cream cone across the table at which she was sitting. She had to be taught everything: how to say "Mommy" and "Daddy" (this may seem to have been presumptuous of the Fitches, but "Mrs. Fitch" and "Mr. Fitch" would have been too much to ask), how to walk (imitation, step by precarious step), how to put food in the mouth instead of eyes, ears, nose, hair and so on.

As in other, similar cases, Harriet learned fast, developed quickly. Soon she was talking, with a rapidly expanding vocabulary. She became comfortable enough with the language to misuse it, childishly. After being chided for letting her dress creep up too high, she passed on the advice to everyone she saw wearing a short skirt or even short sleeves. Having been shown some money about to be spent for ice cream, and so identified, she called money "ice cream" for several days thereafter. Seeing the sun shining through some clouds, she called it a ball—but that's what she called everything that looked round.

Her best environment for rapid learning proved to be the cinema. She loved movies, cheering and applauding and jumping up and down like the matinee-addicted children all about her. (The Fitches had some difficulty keeping her from being conspicuous.) Indeed, according to Susie, the movies were therapeutic, and she recommended that the Fitches keep up the good work. They did, and one evening after a Western, The Baby became quite ill—and Harriet returned. Among other things, she remarked on how much bigger her baby seemed to be. The dissociation had lasted eleven days, and she knew nothing of it.

Harriet remained Harriet from Thursday evening until the next Sunday morning, when she chanced upon a photograph of the dead priest—and she was gone again. This time, however, it was only for a few hours. A hastily summoned Susie informed the Fitches that the problem was lack of blood circulation at the back of the neck, and the need to get it started again was urgent. The Fitches rubbed, kneaded, massaged, even pounded, all without any perceptible effect. Desperately, they tried an electric vibrator. That did it. Suddenly there was Harriet, a worn and weary and ache-all-over but an unmistakable Harriet. From this time on she never again spoke of the priest and even seemed never to think of him. Susie claimed that this was her doing.

Dr. Wholey may have disapproved of the Fitches' generally mystical approach to Harriet's difficulties; he did not say in his report. He clearly admired their sincerity, however, and in the report he described their methods, both physical and spiritual, without any hint of disdain. At any rate, apparently he did not see Harriet for several years until 1929, six years after his first meeting with her. He found her living with George and their four children in an old house in the suburbs. It took her some time to recognize the doctor. When she did, she offered abject apologies and became quite voluble about her recent history and present circumstances.

They had left the home of their befriending couple some 3½ years before. The wife had rather surprisingly become pregnant (it may have been a menopause pregnancy) and, with the arrival of her child, had lost interest in Harriet. In addition, the woman had begun to suspect that her husband's interest in Harriet had passed the stage of exorcism and that Harriet was deliberately mixing in her eros with his agape. Despite her innocence of any such designs, Harriet felt that the time had come to go.

She had survived this rather traumatic experience without dissociating, and she had not dissociated since. She considered herself cured, although she confessed that she never went to movies now lest she get "mixed up" again. She and her husband seemed to have been brought closer together by adversity and by the need to make their own way. The needs of her children, of whom she was very solicitous, had kept shifting the focus of her attention from self to others until now it was more or less a habit. She just didn't need anyone like Susie any more.

The doctor felt that she didn't need him any more, either. He was much impressed with her recovery. As a result of it, he was never to see her again.

Eve White/Chris Costner, 1954

A widely known, extensively documented and spectacular case of multiple personality is that reported by Corbett H. Thigpen and Hervey M. Cleckley in their *The Three Faces of Eve* (McGraw Hill, 1957). The two psychiatrists originally reported the case in the *Journal of Abnormal and Social Psychology* in 1954 and then gave a detailed account in their book, which was later made into a splendid and very popular movie.

They gave their patient the pseudonym of Mrs. Eve White to protect her identity. About twenty years later, however, in a book written by Chris Costner Sizemore and her cousin Elen Sain Pittillo, *I'm Eve* (Doubleday, 1977), the former revealed herself as the famous Eve.

Chris can remember dissociations reaching far back into her childhood. When she was only two, she saw the body of a drowned man hauled from a creek near her home. The timid child, frightened by this first experience with death, then noticed a homely, skinny little girl standing on the small bridge that spanned the creek, and watching the scene quite calmly.

As the years passed, Chris the inhibited had nothing but trouble from this uninhibited other self. Sometimes she would find herself being punished for something she knew nothing about, except for the clear evidence that would be presented to her. At other times she could see the girl and would watch while she engaged in some forbidden act, yet it would be Chris who got the spanking. Her tearful protests that the other girl was the culprit merely earned her a reputation for lying.

Chris loved her parents and received a good deal of loving attention in return as their only child. At the age of six, however, she was suddenly faced with some serious competition in the form of newly arrived twins. She loved them quite dutifully and even sincerely, but her alter ego thoroughly resented the attention lavished on them. On one occasion she expressed this resentment by going up to their bed as they lay asleep and poking her finger in their eyes and giving them a number of hard, disapproving bites on their feet. Her mother, hearing their wails of pain and terror, rushed into the room to find Chris standing over them and staring at their wounds. Chris had *seen* the other girl do this terrible thing, but her protests to that effect were futile. It was her own bottom that got the spanking.

Not long thereafter her grandmother died, and the child's ingrained fear of death was aggravated by an incident at the funeral home that was to be imbedded in her unconscious for many long years to come. As remembered later, the incident began when she and a cousin were playing under the porch and came across the remains of a small blue cup that had belonged to her grandmother. It reminded her of the time when her alter ego had broken it and then retired while Chris suffered the punishment.

While lost in the memory of this instance of painful inequity, she was called to come and say good-bye to Grandma. Standing beside the open coffin, she was lifted by an aunt and instructed to kiss the stiffly pallid face. Terrified at the mere thought of doing any such thing, she screamed and struggled in fierce rebellion until her mother finally came up and rescued her. At the cemetery, still trembling, she watched as the coffin was lowered into the grave. The image of the cold, dark hole might have overcome her if she hadn't seen her counterpart standing beside it, watching the proceedings quite impassively.

But Chris was plagued with nightmares involving her grandmother for the next six months.

School proved to be a sharp disappointment, entailing much more purposeless sitting than the creative activity that she had eagerly, if vaguely, anticipated. Left-handed, she was forced to learn writing with her right hand. But she did become a competent and interested reader, and she even composed a little poetry. Meanwhile her alter ego, spurning the groves and pursuits of academe, often came out to wreak havoc with antics such as pilfering crayons and other supplies from fellow students, thus adding the charge of thief to the reputation for lying that poor Chris had brought from home.

Her school years had some bright moments, but in general they were a severe trial. Her reason for finally dropping out of high school in her senior year was typical: she found herself enrolled in an advanced French class, yet she couldn't remember taking elementary French the year before. Meanwhile other personalities had come and gone, perhaps a dozen of them, but none proved as durable as the girl she had seen first on the bridge.

Life seemed intent on providing Chris with traumatic experiences, including a brutal sexual assault some months after she quit school. Unable to hold a job because of her alter ego's playful irresponsibility, she married, almost in desperation, and soon became pregnant. In January, 1948, her daughter Taffy was born. It was, needless to add, an extremely difficult birth; yet the baby was normal and healthy, and Chris was delighted with her.

But her husband was not so delighted with Chris, whom he found moody and unpredictable. One Saturday evening, pregnant again, she begged him so insistently not to go out that he became impatient and, during the altercation, accidentally struck her in the face. Not realizing the force of the blow, he left, whereupon she collapsed and had a miscarriage. She lay where she fell, dazed and bleeding, until her parents happened by for a visit the following afternoon.

After this she was plagued with headaches, blackouts and voices—especially a persistent voice indulging in bitter vituperation against her husband and sometimes forcing her to take violent action. On two occasions, to protect Taffy from severe punishment, she threatened him with his own gun. Even more alarmingly, the voice seemed to be taking on an intermittent life of its own: more and more often, Chris would emerge from a blackout to find herself in some unaccountable predicament.

Her parents, sharing her alarm, took her to a doctor, who urgently recommended a visit to a psychiatric clinic. This was the advice that led her to a series of visits with Dr. Thigpen.

During one of her early visits, Chris complained of hearing a woman's voice speaking to her. This caused the doctor some concern, since he knew that "auditory hallucinations" usually were associated with psychosis. Yet this patient's attitude toward the voice was that of a mentally normal, not a psychotic, person. She was by no means sure that the voice really existed, for instance, and she was terribly worried that her hearing it might mean that she could be losing her mind. Then one day while the doctor, impressed by the sanity of her reactions, was trying to reassure her, the sober Chris White suddenly went into a kind of catatonic state for a moment, and then Chris Black emerged, with sparkling eyes and a merry grin. "Hi there, Doc!" she exclaimed.

For several months thereafter the doctor carried on conversations alternately with the diffident Chris White (who knew little or nothing about Chris Black) and the boisterous Chris Black (who knew everything about Chris White, and incidentally didn't like her much). To talk with Chris Black, he would hypnotize Chris White and "call out" Chris Black; to reverse the process he would simply ask Chris Black, whom he could never hypnotize, to bring Chris White back. The necessity for hypnosis diminished as time passed, and before long the transformations, either way, required only simple requests. As the conversations continued, Chris White's health seemed to improve: her anxiety abated somewhat, and the headaches that had plagued her became less frequent and intense. Before long, however, she suffered a relapse, and even the irrepressible Chris Black began showing signs of uncertainty and uneasiness. By now the doctor had become so intimately acquainted with them both that he was all the more astonished when they both unexpectedly receded and a third personality emerged.

She introduced herself, hesitantly and doubtfully, as Jane. She had emerged without any knowledge of either Chris, of the doctor, or her own or anyone else's history. (The doctor later learned, for instance, that she didn't know who George Washington was, and some months thereafter she mentioned that, having experienced winter and spring, she was eagerly looking forward to seeing what summer would be like.) Yet, unlike the newly reborn Thomas Hanna, she spoke English well (better than either Chris) and displayed a kind of compassionate wisdom normally associated with a long-established maturity. Like Thomas Hanna, she learned facts very quickly, and over the next several months she gradually became the dominant personality.

None too soon. Before Jane's arrival, the frolicsome Chris Black had grown quite literally irrepressible. Sometimes she would come out in the afternoon, change her clothes (she had squirreled away a limited but rakishly colorful wardrobe for her outings) and then take off on a pleasure jaunt, usually at one of the local cocktail lounges or nightclubs. Taffy was simply left at home to shift for herself. On one of these occasions the husband arrived home to find that the child had fallen and hurt her leg. When Chris Black showed up several hours later in her flashy cocktail dress and with the smell of liquor on her breath, he nearly went berserk. The next morning, of course, Chris White remembered nothing about the episode, but her husband's impassioned account of it, combined with her own awareness of a blackout, did nothing to maintain her peace of mind.

Promoting her peace of mind was hardly very high on Chris Black's list of priorities. On one of her more spectacular shopping sprees, for example, she spent most of a day at several downtown stores, selecting a budget-smashing supply of fancy lingerie, shoes, stockings and evening gowns, and an expensive coat. Returning home in the midafternoon, she cheerfully stashed her loot in a closet, closed the door, and then turned things over to her unsuspecting double. Unfortunately it was the husband who, on coming home from work, went to the closet first, so that Chris White's introduction to her new, husband-harrowing wardrobe came in the form of alarming questions addressed to her in very alarmed tones.

She was astounded, of course, and totally at a loss to explain how those fancy things had managed to get into the closet. She made almost all her own clothes, and what little she bought would never look anything like *that*! But her husband could hardly be blamed for rejecting the notion that the new contents of the closet had somehow convened there under their own power. She agreed that the circumstantial evidence was undeniable (as usual, she was vaguely aware of a blackout period which she resisted admitting even to herself), and she promised fervently to do everything she could to return the booty and have the charges canceled.

Her efforts to do so were only partly successful. As a result Chris Black, as she told the doctor later, at least was spared the humiliation of having to wear those colorless, drab, mousy and very respectable skirts and blouses to which Chris White was so demurely addicted. A girl with any spirit, after all, can't go around looking like the town librarian.

She often could be quite adroit at her comings and goings. For example, as she told the doctor during an interview, if her double were downtown shopping and looked at something in a display window (usually at something for Taffy, to Chris Black's intense chagrin), the hoyden would take the opportunity to come out for a quarter of an hour or so, wander down to the local drugstore-hangout, indulge in a soft drink and some kidding, return to the display window and, while staring at it, go back in. Chris White would thus, at most, be only dimly aware that a blackout might have occurred.

The procedure didn't always work out quite so smoothly. Another time she unexpectedly discovered herself talking with a strange soldier on a downtown street. Come on, he insisted, let's go right now. His condition of eager impatience was pretty clearly one for which Chris White would not have known the appropriate word. She firmly declined. Puzzled, he pleaded with her. She continued to decline, still firmly but so quietly and modestly that the soldier finally gave up in stupefied frustration.

Chris Black explained the incident in a later interview with the doctor. She had met the soldier, whom she knew, quite by chance and had agreed to a date with him that evening. Encouraged by her compliance, he insisted on an immediate "date," the nature of which was soon clear to her. When she declined, he continued to insist so vigorously that she thought for a moment of making a scene to get rid of him. Then the ideal solution occurred to her, and Chris White once again found herself in the role of patsy.

But gradually the hoyden's appearance became more than merely embarrassing. One weekend, emerging while Chris White was cleaning some window blinds, she launched into an abusive argument with her husband, frightening Taffy to tears. Thoroughly annoyed, she called the child a brat and began coiling the window-blind cord tightly about her throat. When the husband came to the rescue, she retreated and left to poor Chris White the impossible task of explanation.

On one occasion, however, she did prove to be of some value. In a fit of deep despondency one day, Chris White tried to slash her wrists but was prevented by the emergence of Chris Black, who immediately wrote the doctor a note reporting the incident. And Chris White was hospitalized for a while.

It was not long after this that Jane appeared, but her arrival, despite her quickness to learn, proved no instant cure-all. She and Chris White had to resign from several jobs because of Chris Black's incorrigible penchant for goofing up and goofing off. Indeed, eventually the personnel manager of a large department store told her that she would probably never be hired by any firm in town because her reputation (for having "a strange illness") now preceded her at employment offices.

Meanwhile Chris White, her marriage having deteriorated beyond repair, filed for divorce. Jane had concurred in this decision, and of course Chris Black was delighted. As a result, after the legal papers had been drawn up, there was no problem about agreement. But the signing ceremony, as was now the case in any legal proceeding involving Chris, was no ordinary event. Through an arrangement that the doctor had made with an extraordinarily unflappable attorney, all three personalities signed the divorce papers.

Some weeks later Jane met Don Sizemore. On this particular evening she was standing unattended for a moment at a party when a young man asked her for a dance. She replied diffidently that she didn't dance well and suggested that he ask her roommate, standing nearby. No, he persisted, he wanted to dance with *her*.

They danced. They talked, They spent the evening together, They began dating. Things grew quite serious, and Jane told him about her peculiar problem. It made no difference, he said. They were definitely in love.

This relationship continued to deepen, but Jane's condition took a very alarming turn. Now *she* began having headaches and nightmares. Then one day, while playing catch with Taffy in the grandparents' front yard, she had to crawl under the porch to retrieve the ball. A feeling suddenly seized her that she had done this before, but without any stooping. There was something dreamlike in the situation, as though, like Alice in Wonderland, she had eaten a biscuit that had made her tall. After she found the ball and brought it back out, the feeling subsided.

But it stayed with her in the sense that she attached great significance to it. This was obvious to the doctor as she described the incident in their next interview. It was an unusual interview, for all three personalities seemed on edge. Even Chris Black was uneasy; indeed, she used the word "scared" at one point and asked the doctor rather pathetically if "we" would *ever* get well. Then, shortly after Jane's description of her experience under the porch, he asked to talk to Chris White. Jane grew rigid, her eyes widened in fright. She began to whimper, begging that she not, *not* be made to do it. And then she screamed. Oh, how she screamed!

Thoroughly alarmed, Dr. Thigpen rushed from his office to get Dr. Cleckley. When the two men returned a moment later, the patient was calmer but disoriented. Yet despite her confusion, and theirs, both men sensed immediately that this was a fourth personality whom they had never met. After she had grown calm enough to respond, they asked her who she was. She didn't know, she answered; she wasn't sure.

She exhibited none of Chris White's painful diffidence, none of Chris Black's impish exuberance. Although she most closely resembled Jane, she remembered past events not as part of her own separate past but rather as things that had happened to the three other personalities. Gradually, as she grew still calmer and the interview progressed, she recognized that somehow she had an identity of her own. When the doctor asked to speak with Chris White, she realized that Chris White was gone, and so was Chris Black. Had Chris Costner finally come into her own?

Not yet, unfortunately. For some weeks after her marriage to Don Sizemore, she seemed quite normal, basking in his consideration and patience. The home they bought, however, because Don's construction work was likely to keep them on the move, was a mobile home. It was comfortable enough and perfectly respectable, but Chris tended to associate "trailers" with a kind of rootless existence that she abhorred. This may have aggravated her chronic insecurity. Whatever the reason, she was soon having problems again—and giving them.

The first serious indication that she wasn't well came during an argument with a woman who lived in the next trailer, over the destruction of some toys of Taffy's. Perhaps significantly, it was when the woman called her a liar that Chris lost her temper. She punched the woman in the face, jumped on her as she lay fallen, bit her on the legs, grabbed her hair and pounded her head on the floor like a mallet, and generally treated her to greater vehemence than the battered woman could possibly have bargained for. When Don, called from work, arrived to quiet the storm, she had calmed down enough for embarrassed contrition, although her reason for embarrassment seemed to be merely that her conduct had been less than ladylike.

Soon thereafter the Sizemores moved to another trailer court.

At their new location the good news was that Chris, after volunteering to help out at Taffy's school, performed so well that the principal asked her to become a regular substitute teacher. The bad news was that Furman University, in response to her letter requesting a transcript of her credits, wrote her that no record existed of her ever having attended any classes there. She hadn't, of course, but her admired cousin Elen had, and Chris had simply indulged in some wishful identification. That ended her substitute teaching career.

And it did nothing to promote her precarious equanimity. One day, provoked by the loud audio from a television program that Taffy was watching, she let go with a butcher knife in the general direction of the TV set, missing it widely, and then sank to the floor in a dead faint. When she came to, she was lying on a couch, with Don bending solicitously over her, but she couldn't see him. She had gone blind, and she stayed blind until the next morning when Don was driving her to an eye doctor. The doctor, after learning that she had gone temporarily blind and that her eyes still hurt, prescribed a pair of low-power reading glasses. Astonishingly, she continued to go blind now and then, but the glasses, quite dependably, would restore her vision.

Don, Chris and Taffy were destined to live through this sort of thing for the next twenty years—headaches, sleeplessness, fainting spells, blackouts, suicide attempts, and perhaps as many as a dozen different personalities. These included the woman who went blind under stress; loving and kind, and able to enjoy sex, she nevertheless suffered from anxiety and excessive dependency on others. There were also the competent but too protective woman who obsessively collected bells, the woman who collected turtle figurines, the woman who collected playing cards, the elderly woman who wore only purple, and the two impish girls, one with an uncontrollable passion for strawberries, the other with a similar passion for banana splits. And there was the anxious, prissy woman who, considering herself an unmarried virgin, refused to sleep with Don.

The family held together by dint of remarkable patience and loving solicitude. Taffy, as she grew older, was especially helpful and supportive. So was cousin Elen, whose work with Chris in writing *I'm Eve* may have offered better therapy than any conceivable alternative. And so were the physician and psychiatrist who treated Chris in her middle years. Both refused to deal with any other personalities, treating Chris simply as a single patient.

By 1977, the manuscript had been completed and sent to the publisher, and Chris Costner Sizemore had emerged from the effort a seemingly free and stable personality. Whatever her remaining uncertainties, she now felt a more solid and reassuring hope than she had ever known before.

Gloria, 1972

In March, 1972, *Comprehensive Psychiatry* published an article by two very skeptical psychiatrists, Drs. Paul Horton and Derek Miller, of the University of Michigan Medical Center. In their introductory statement they pointed out the possibility that another personality may be merely an "artifact of investigation," created by the patient at the unintended suggestion of an overeager therapist. William James, they added, had been similarly doubtful about some of Pierre Janet's diagnoses. But recently they had observed a case of multiple personality in which suggestion by the therapist apparently played no part.

In their article they did not consider other possible sources of such suggestion. Perhaps for this reason the case presented, that of a girl named Gloria, is relatively unconvincing. Multiple personalities were vividly portrayed in two movies issued in the late fifties, when Gloria was in her infancy: *The Three Faces of Eve* and *Lizzie*, the latter based on a story by Shirley Jackson of *The Lost Weekend* fame. Shown in later years as television reruns, both movies depict personalities very similar to those revealed by Gloria. Another unusual feature of the case is that Gloria very explicitly, repeatedly, and eagerly referred to what she herself called her "split personalities" long before the therapist acceded to the diagnosis. The suggestion involved seems to have been all on *her* side, and suspiciously so.

For all this, her previous history provided enough reason for accepting the case as genuine. Her mother was a rather frosty, remote individual who spoke of the four children more often by number than by name. The father was an unreliable breadwinner, a wifebeater and a tireless adulterer. According to Gloria, he had some sort of sexual relations with his oldest daughter. At the age of ten, Gloria overheard her father's end of a telephone conversation with a girl friend, which he interrupted with a request that he be given a minute to "get rid of the brat." In the mother's presence he was, or pretended to be, considerate of the children, often protecting them from her punishments; if this was merely an act, it surely didn't fool the children. Gloria's younger sister wet the bed regularly (at age thirteen) and was generally "difficult," while her still younger brother moped about in a state of depression and wistfully hoped for escape.

After the father's desertion of the family, he provided them with regular financial support but with very little support of any other kind. Gloria would have to plead with him to grant her an occasional visit. She could not explain why she did so, since she professed only hatred for the man. But before long this was not the only aspect of her behavior that was hard to explain, for she was soon suffering from severe headaches, distortion of vision, hallucinations, suicidal impulses, sleepwalking, and spells of fainting and difficult breathing. Her father appeared in her hallucinations with the body of a monster. Another aspect of her illness was garrulity, displayed in rather disconnected, shallow monologues, often accompanied by behavior that contradicted her words, as in her tossing off a despairing remark with a laugh. Still another aspect was thievery, but with a multiple-personality twist: pilfering from her sisters without any memory later of having done so. This last, of course, is a very common sort of occurrence in multiple-personality cases, and indeed her own testimony was that she began dissociating soon after her father's departure.

Her family doctor, feeling that her symptoms were a little more than he could handle, sent her to a neurologist for further diagnosis. The neurologist turned up nothing clearly significant except a possible indication of epilepsy in her electroencephalogram, an indication that he could not pursue because of her failure to come back for additional testing. It was his recommendation of psychiatric treatment that brought her to the Medical Center, where the mother also agreed to undergo therapy concurrently. Gloria was now sixteen.

At the Center her condition was diagnosed as psychosis, probably a paranoid schizophrenia. The possibility that the psychosis might be hysterical rather than schizophrenic was recognized but dismissed as inconsequential to the decision on type of treatment, which would be the same in either case. A daily dose of six milligrams of Stelazine was prescribed, and over the next eight months Gloria's psychiatric sessions averaged about two hours per month. As her hallucinations and suicidal deliberations diminished, she seemed to change personality, becoming something of an adolescent version of Eve White—plain, dull, quiet, often painfully shy, devoted to music, prone to compulsive behavior. She complained of being abused by her sisters and of being accused, like Eve White, of doing things that she was sure she hadn't done. She had a boy friend, she said, a young stalwart with whom she rollerskated and attended church. This girl, according to Gloria's later testimony, was named Debby.

After the fourth session the patient felt that she was well enough to discontinue treatment and to rely solely on the Stelazine, a course that appealed to her as less costly. She was persuaded otherwise, however, and—perhaps because of a growing confidence in Dr. Horton— revealed another personality. In the immediately following sessions Debby gave way to Carolyn, an adolescent version of Eve Black—a brash, irascible but thoroughly alluring hoyden who enhanced her charms with colorful cosmetics and engagingly brief attire and who pressed the doctor for interesting information about his wife. She described uninhibited parties that she went to late at night, implying various intimacies with the men that she met there. Although she seemed to enjoy this life on the surface, she was soon regressing. She discontinued taking the Stelazine and shortly thereafter began again to suffer from hallucinations, unpredictable swoons, and sometimes seizure-like attacks. It was at about this time that she first brought up the notion of "split personalities."

At this time, too, Gloria described a fourth personality, Susan, whom the doctor hadn't met but who, she said, had really been the first to emerge, immediately after her father had left for warmer hearths. Susan seems to have been modeled on an attractive, gregarious, successful schoolmate who had a normal, mutually affectionate relationship with her father. Gloria's descriptions of this relationship were heavily laced with bitter irony.

The revelation of the various personalities seemed to have a cathartic effect. Gloria's condition improved enough to elicit praise from friends. She grew more introspective and thus more self-controlled. She got herself a job and began taking correspondence courses in an effort to finish high school. But she and her mother discontinued their treatment, both pleading inability to take time off from work. Dr. Horton offered to make some mutually convenient arrangement, and on four occasions during the next thirty weeks or so one or another of the personalities phoned in a request for an appointment. But in each instance, soon thereafter Gloria phoned in a cancellation. The life of a psychiatrist is not without its frustrations.

Carmen Garcia, 1973

Carmen Garcia was a patient of Dr. Robert J. Stoller, a highly reputable California psychiatrist who has described her case in detail in his book, *Splitting* (New York Times Book Company, 1973). Her name here of course is fictitious, chosen because of her fluency in both English and Spanish and because her first name was one of those that are about as common among men as among women.

Dr. Stoller treated Carmen for about ten years, from her mid-twenties to her mid-thirties. She had an unusual history of behavior, to say the least. At the age of four she had nearly killed a little boy with a rock. As an adult, she had shot a policeman and a male friend (the latter five times). She had injured and almost killed a man in a clearly contrived auto "accident." She had tried to stab her husband and later had tried to poison him. She had nearly dispatched two of her sons, with gas and drugs, in an abortive attempt at murder and suicide. On other, separate occasions, she had been prevented from shooting a school principal, her husband, and even Dr. Stoller himself.

That isn't all, by any means. She was a very busy person. By the time of her referral to the doctor, she had set dozens of fires, robbed half a dozen gas stations, stolen three cars, passed a number of bad checks, participated in a couple of pornographic films, and consummated countless affairs with men (some of them members of the family) and some twenty with women. She had been married four times and illegitimately pregnant five times. She had often taken heroin and had been addicted to amphetamine half a dozen times. Her associations were largely criminal, and her auto traffic record was a wonder to behold.

Her father teased her a great deal as a child, and her mother evidently was a very severe and disapproving martinet. The household rang, for instance, with admonitions on what "ladies" do and don't do in a polite society. Although she was not a battered child by any means, or even a deprived one, family pressures were heavy enough for her to seek comfort from a leprechaun that a much beloved uncle had told her about. She kept the leprechaun for several years, talking with him and seeking his advice and moral support, until David appeared.

David came to be known as Charlie in her discussions with the doctor, for trivial reasons having to do with the Charlie Brown comic strip. Charlie was the boy she wanted to be. Among her peculiarities was her conviction that she had a penis, a perfectly serviceable organ, hidden inside her. As an imaginary companion, Charlie might have been considered merely a projection of the desperate wish represented by the penis, yet he was more, much more. Indeed, he tried to argue Carmen out of her hallucination, pointing out that having an imaginary penis was as futile as having an imaginary dog that no one else could see or hear. But when the doctor asked her if Charlie wasn't right about this, she replied no, that you can't feel an imaginary dog inside you.

To the doctor's surprise, Charlie was present for Carmen regardless of her mental condition at the time. He was there when her behavior was normal as well as when it was psychotic. He could be very demanding. Sometimes he was so insistent on having her undivided attention that she couldn't hear anyone else talking to her. On occasion the doctor would complain, with a comment like "You're not listening to me, you're listening to Charlie!" and she would agree, often relaying what Charlie had said.

Charlie was what most people would call an evil influence, except perhaps in his declining years. His first words to her, Carmen told the doctor, were "Hit him!" She was four at the time and playing innocently near her home with a little boy, in a hole dug by some of the neighborhood children. Suddenly feeling a need to urinate, the boy satisfied it immediately, there in the hole, and Carmen found this solution to his problem very distressing. It also made her very envious. So when she heard Charlie's voice saying "Hit him," she hit the boy on the head with a rock. The boy fled, yelping with pain. And she got a whipping.

Many years later, in a conversation with the doctor, she expressed some doubt about Charlie's role in this incident. It was so long ago. But she was in no doubt at all about later incidents in which he tried to kill her, or make her kill herself, once with an overdose of a drug and once by getting her to ram her car into an immovable wall at an irresistible 65 miles per hour. He also was behind her attempt to kill herself and her children with overdoses of sleeping tablets. (As it turned out, there weren't enough to go around, they all survived, and she was remanded to a state hospital.) Nor was Carmen in any doubt about Charlie's seductively urging her into homosexual affairs, despite the fact that at other times he would ridicule her as a "stupid queer." On other aspects of her unflagging sex life, however, he expressed no opinion, either way.

Charlie had a good side, especially as he and Carmen grew older. He could be very comforting when she was in trouble and depressed. He would often cheer her up with items from his teeming repertoire of Spanish jokes. (He spoke better Spanish than she, and better English too. And, she said, he was smarter.) His thorough dislike for her mother often brought her solace, and in the early years he afforded some protection by persuading her not to feel things so intensely. In this he was too successful, and in their later years he had to reverse himself. The insensitivity that had protected her as a child got her into all kinds of trouble as an adult.

As the treatment progressed, the doctor found that Charlie was becoming more helpful to him as well as to Carmen, that he seemed to be mellowing with increasing maturity. It was Charlie, Carmen reported, who had advised her to enter into her fourth and most successful (or least unsuccessful) marriage. He was telling her now, almost like St. Paul, to put the things of childhood behind her, to rely on him less, to stand on her own against the vicissitudes of life. As he grew more aware that the doctor did not want simply to eliminate him but rather wanted the integration of his and Carmen's personalities, his advice to Carmen became increasingly like the doctor's own. Carmen grew more comfortable with this advice, slowly coming to the realization that Charlie's opinions were her own. Eventually the integration was complete, and Charlie departed almost imperceptibly from her life.

In the meantime, however, the doctor had discovered that Carmen and Charlie were not alone. About midway in the treatment he became conscious of another personality who operated much differently from Charlie. Carmen, he learned, experienced rather frequent blackouts, which psychiatrists call "fugues." During these blackouts she would do things, usually "bad things," which she later could not remember doing. The most serious of the fires that she had caused, for instance, had almost destroyed her home. Later she recalled everything that occurred immediately before the setting of the fire, in the garage, and everything immediately thereafter. Yet she had no memory whatsoever of actually starting the fire, admitting that she must have done so only because the circumstantial evidence was undeniable. (A significant childhood memory was of her mother's frequent comment that there was a part of Carmen that she simply didn't understand.)

In discussing the fire with her, the doctor, seizing on a sudden insight, asked if there was "another you" who could have started the fire. Why, yes, she replied, there was "the quiet one," who unlike Charlie didn't talk to her but who sometimes got angry or otherwise excited and who might then take over and do a bad thing that Carmen afterward wouldn't remember doing. This other personality was a woman. Unlike Charlie (or David), she had no name that Carmen was aware of. She never spoke to Carmen, who nevertheless was usually dimly conscious of her presence. She was more gregarious, often taking over when Carmen was in a bar or cocktail lounge, especially when Carmen was with a man whom she (the quiet one) found attractive. What her relations with such men might be Carmen could only guess, since for her these periods were simply blackouts. But occasionally she found postcoital evidence . . . .

As the intermittent discussions of Carrie continued ("Carrie," the doctor was to learn, was what she called herself), he began to suspect that her memory of childhood events was much better than Carmen's. One way to plumb this reservoir of vital information, he felt, might be through hypnosis. He broached the idea to Carmen, but she seemed so shaken by the suggestion that he withdrew it. Yet curiously it seemed to bring Carrie closer to the surface. And then one day, quite unexpectedly, he got a phone call. It was from Carrie.

The call lasted half an hour. The conversation was brisk but cordial, casual but enlightening. Carrie was brighter than Carmen, as well as happier. And, as the doctor had suspected, her memory was nearly faultless.

This was only the first of many such calls over the next several weeks. Carrie had decided, she told the doctor, to take over much more often than she had in the past. She had done so before, however, simply to indulge herself; now she was doing so in an effort to help Carmen. But it soon became clear that her efforts were having quite an opposite effect. She was taking over so frequently that Carmen became chronically uncertain and mixed up and even began to be vaguely aware of what Carrie was doing during the blackouts. Although this development had its hopeful aspects, Carmen was becoming so disoriented and depressed that the doctor was seriously alarmed.

The day finally arrived when Carrie and the doctor met face to face. By this time Carmen could talk with Carrie, somewhat as she had with the now departed Charlie, usually in a silent (or at least inaudible) communion. At this particular session the doctor made a request of Carmen: ask Carrie to take over and talk with me, but you stay in the background and listen to our conversation. Carmen agreed to try, rather nervously. Her eyes went blank, and then Carrie introduced herself.

Her name, she explained by way of introduction, was the name that her mother had wanted to give her. Her grandmother, evidently a formidable woman, insisted on naming her after her father. Perhaps as a result of this sort of family pressure, Carmen always hated being a female and made up for it in a number of ways.

Carrie had surfaced for the first time at about the age of five, she thought, although she could remember some things that had happened as early as two. Like Charlie, she had not been a very good influence. She had often (though by no means always) been responsible for Carmen's playing hooky and for her aberrant behavior as an adult. (She frequently felt guilty, she reported, but Carmen never did.) She despised Carmen's fourth husband, and it was she who had almost burnt down the house by setting fire to some treasured political papers of his, partly in the hope of forcing a separation or divorce. On another occasion she had taken over for a whole weekend, during which she went to San Francisco and squandered $500 on the family credit card. (Carmen didn't know about this because the husband, who evidently was patient and tolerant almost beyond belief, simply said nothing about the bills he later received. She had told him before they were married that she was capable of doing crazy things.)

Carrie's behavior was generally impulsive but not always self-indulgent. Like Charlie, she was good for Carmen on occasion. One of Carmen's children, a boy, had reached the age of 17 months without showing any signs of learning to walk or talk. Convinced that Carmen was simply refusing to accept clear evidence that he was retarded and needed special treatment, Carrie took over one day and drove the child to the office of a specialist in town for an examination. During the examination she retreated, leaving Carmen to hear the doctor tell her that the boy probably was retarded. Although she at first continued in her refusal to believe any such thing, Carmen did take him to a psychologist, a personal friend, who gave the same opinion, and eventually she came to accept the truth, to the child's considerable benefit as well as her own.

Carrie's sessions with the doctor, combined with Carmen's, went on for the next couple of months. He made it clear to them both that his purpose was to bring them together. Carrie was quite willing to cooperate, but Carmen was nervous, even frightened, at the thought of spending the rest of her life without either Charlie or Carrie. As the conversations continued, however, the line of demarcation between Carmen and Carrie began to blur. During the conversations Carmen began to say things that sounded like Carrie. She became more relaxed, more willing to enjoy life. And her memory improved enormously. She and Carrie "grew together," as Charlie had long ago recommended, and Carmen was much more a whole and happy person than she had ever been. And Carrie joined Charlie in the realm of recollection.

Sybil Dorsett, 1973

Sybil Dorsett was a girl with a secret. She kept it strictly to herself because she was ashamed and frightened. The secret was that she had what she called "blank spells." They were frequent, occupying perhaps a third of her waking hours, and they lasted anywhere from a few minutes to several days—one, during her childhood, lasted almost two years. Although she had no memory of what happened during any of these blackouts, she was always aware that *something* had happened because her family and friends would refer to things she had done as though she naturally knew about them too. Sometimes she was punished for misbehavior of which she had no recollection whatsoever. She felt certain she hadn't done those things, yet as time went on she gradually realized that she could never be *really* certain. She became withdrawn and timid, and always unsure of herself.

Her story has been told quite eloquently by Flora Rheta Schreiber in a fascinating, controversial book, *Sybil* (Regnery, 1973). It is a case of multiple personality carried to unprecedented extremes. From about the age of three and for about forty years thereafter, Sybil's body was intermittently inhabited by sixteen different people.

Different *people*? Surely, one may protest, that's a bit much. Sixteen different aspects of the same person, perhaps, but not sixteen people! The answer to this is less than crystal clear because it all depends on how one defines "person"—and no one can, at least with any precision and finality. Yet it's significant that the psychiatrists who have treated cases of multiple personality—and who have had wide experience with the vivid but clearly imaginary personalities created in daydreams and hallucinations—often, if not usually, have not been quite sure just which of the personalities was the "real" one.

It has become a cliche in psychiatry that pathological behavior in an adult will most probably have its roots in some childhood experience or experiences, and Sybil's case proved no exception. She was an only

119

child, born rather precariously (her mother had had several miscarriages) when her parents were in their forties. The Wisconsin town of her childhood, called Willow Corners to conceal yet characterize its identity for the public record, was something right out of the pages of Sinclair Lewis. Predominantly fundamentalist, secure in the favor of God and the unerring prescriptions of the Bible, dedicated to a morality consisting mainly of disapproval of others, contemptuous of nonconformity, it provided for its children an American Gothic atmosphere redolent with the proprieties of the conditioned reflex. Although it was by no means the root cause of Sybil's problems, it helped to reinforce the religious hangups that plagued her throughout her life.

Sybil's mother, Hattie, had had four brothers and eight sisters. In such large families, depending partly on the atmosphere created by the parents, there can be an abundance of love, but from Hattie's overworked mother there was chiefly neglect. (Many of the children developed psychological and psychosomatic problems as adults.) Perhaps in compensation, Hattie devoted herself to her schoolwork, becoming a consistent A student and especially developing her musical talent to the point where her teachers enthusiastically recommended that she be sent to a music conservatory for training as a concert pianist.

And so Hattie set her heart on a musical career, dreaming of a future in which she would be a rich and famous concert star. But it was not to be. One evening when she was twelve her father, who owned a prosperous music store, informed her that she wouldn't be going to school the next day; she would begin working in his store, replacing an older sister who was soon to be married. Hattie knew that this represented a quite unnecessary economy, but she was not about to rebel openly against the paternal tyranny. Riven with disappointment, she couldn't even cry, for crying was frowned on most severely. Instead she laughed, shrilly and hysterically. That wild laugh was to characterize her for the rest of her life.

Not long thereafter she became afflicted with a case of St. Vitus' Dance so severe that ordinary household noises could send her into a frenzy. More enduring was her deep-seated hatred for her father. While he was alive she expressed this hatred (though only occasionally) in such acts as cutting up his favorite smoking jacket, embarrassing him in church, and tattling on his efforts to ease the pain of a terminal illness with liquor. Yet at other times, and especially after his death, she idolized him—expressing *this* attitude, for instance, by keeping his replacement smoking jacket in a chest throughout her life and fondling it during fits of nostalgia. Hating one's father must be denied even to one-self, of course, for it is against the Lord's commandment, especially in places like Willow Corners.

Similarly, she remembered her mother with sentimental admiration, although the woman's most estimable quality seems to have been wifely acquiescence. All the children of the family exhibited various degrees of neurotic behavior in their adult lives. As for poor Hattie, she was schizophrenic (a Mayo Clinic diagnosis) by the time she was forty, when Sybil was born.

Willard Dorsett, Sybil's father, also came from a father-dominated household. His father, indeed, was a militantly religious nut with an obsessive fear of Roman Catholicism and a weirdly personal fundamentalism which demanded of his three children, for instance, that they always smile (for smiling was Christian) but never laugh (for laughing was a sin). As a boy Willard was both sensitive and sensible enough to be embarrassed by his father's Christian hostilities and idiocies, but he was weak enough to share them as an adult. He became an interesting mixture, for part of him—from his mother, perhaps—was quite humanistic, displaying an interest in music and other arts and leading him into a successful career as a small-town architect. This part of him was never quite at ease with the fixed-smile, pious xenophobia instilled in him by his formidably dotty father. Even during his fourteen-year break from the church, he scrupulously observed its myriad "shall not" regulations.

Perhaps this ambivalence made him indecisive in dealing with his wife and her treatment of their child. He by no means knew everything there was to know about that treatment, but this was chiefly because he found it easier to ignore the physical evidence than to pursue it and confront her with it. This was, after all, some forty years before the "battered child" problem was officially recognized, and he could hardly be expected to embrace evidence that flatly contradicted his most sacred bedrock beliefs about motherhood, any more than he could be expected to harbor doubts about apple pie.

Partly because of his willing ignorance, Sybil was a badly battered child, for Hattie was a very sick woman. It was not merely a matter of cruel and unusual punishments, with quite visible results in the form of black eyes, large and colorful bruises, fractures and dislocations. Such treatment was the milder aspect of Sybil's upbringing. Much more traumatic were the effects of Hattie's compulsive sadism, which almost daily made the child's preschool life a living hell. It included binding the little girl in various ways and doing such things as forcing cold water up her urethra and into her bladder; giving her unnecessary, adult-size enemas and forcing her to retain the water until she was in agony with cramps; inserting assorted objects—little boxes, bottles, knives, button-hooks, her fingers—into Sybil's vagina with such force and frequency that Sybil was told by a gynecologist some twenty years later that the damage would prevent her from ever having children; and making her drink a large glass of milk of magnesia, demanding that she go to bed rather than to the bathroom, and then beating her for soiling the bed. And to such basic activities the frenzied mother added variations. Filling the child's bladder with cold water, for instance, often was just a prelude to tying her fast to a leg of the piano and torturing her with the heavy vibrations of a Chopin polonaise. In addition, there were persistent little "accidents"—tripping the child and causing her to fall downstairs, dropping things on her (a rolling pin, a hot iron), slamming a drawer on her hand. Not a few of these tricks were quite dangerous— as when the child was left in a wheat crib and almost smothered to death—and it is surprising that Sybil survived at all, as well as downright amazing that she survived without completely losing her mind. She seems to have had an inner strength. Hattie doubtless would have explained that the child came from good stock.

But Sybil avoided psychosis at the price of hysteria. By about the age of three she couldn't take any more. Her personality split asunder. Three people emerged, though neither Sybil nor her mother knew of their emergence. The daughter's suppressed rage against her mother found expression in the person of Peggy Lou, a rather aggressive young lady who treated Hattie with much less reverence and at times even with some open hostility. (Hattie had recently taken to calling Sybil by the name of Peggy, or Peggy Louisiana, more often than not.) Sybil's fear—indeed, her terror, which had become too much for her to handle alone—was entrusted to Peggy Ann, who evidently cringed a lot. But by far the most interesting of the three newcomers was Vicky, or Victoria Antoinette Scharleau, a cool little blonde who airily dismissed Hattie and Willard as Sybil's parents (and perhaps Peggy Lou's and Peggy Ann's, although those two girls were careful to call themselves Baldwin—Sybil had liked a teacher named Miss Baldwin). As for Vicky's parents, they were in Europe, living mostly in Paris, and they would return before long, bringing her love and security. Meanwhile she would enjoy life whenever Sybil's circumstances would permit. For as time passed she became aware of having an important advantage over Sybil and the Peggys. Sybil knew nothing of the other personalities, even of their existence; she was aware only of her "blank spells," which sometimes left behind evidence that puzzled her as much as her blank-spell behavior puzzled her mother ("Honestly, sometimes she just acts like another person!"). The Peggys knew each other quite intimately and Vicky somewhat more distantly; they seem to have had, at best, uncertain control over their emergences, which ordinarily (if that's a meaningful word under these circumstances) would occur when Sybil was experiencing an intense if unconscious reaction of anger or fear. Vicky, however, knew everything about everyone (including all the later personalities) and exercised considerable control over her own and the others' emergences. Indeed, during analysis years later, she often seemed the "real" personality instead of Sybil.

By her twenty-first birthday Sybil had accumulated eleven more personalities. They were all quite distinct not only in character but, as they saw it, even in appearance. About a year after the first emergence of Vicky and the Peggys, Marcia Lynn Dorsett appeared on the scene. Very artistic and highly emotional, she was a painter like Sybil and a writer as well. Another year later, in 1928, four more emerged: Sybil Ann Dorsett, a languid, painfully diffident, colorless ash blonde; Marjorie Dorsett, a happy, mischievous, lithe and lively little brunette; Mike Dorsett, a rather swarthy young carpenter with Willard Dorsett's fascination with building things; and Sid Dorsett, a more Nordic version of Mike, with less devotion to building and more interest in repair and maintenance. Both these young gentlemen were male chauvinists who simply would not admit their obvious genital deficiency.

In 1929, Helen Dorsett appeared. Brown-haired and hazel-eyed, she displayed in the set of her thin lips the tension between her fear and her determination. The year 1933 brought out Mary Lucinda Dorsett, a rather chubby, motherly type with strong religious feelings. And 1935 introduced a redhead, Vanessa Gail Dorsett, a fetching young lady with a flair for the dramatic. Of indeterminate date were three others: Nancy Lou Ann Baldwin, like the Peggys in appearance but like Grandfather Dorsett in her religious opinions; Clara Dorsett, whose fanatically religious views were expressed mostly in severe disapproval of others, especially Sybil; and Ruthie Dorsett, infantile and the least developed of the fifteen personalities. The sixteenth, a nameless blonde teenager, did not appear until 1946.

Sybil's first dissociation occurred in September, 1926, when she was 3½. She had been taken to a hospital with a very sore throat. The doctor identified her problem as tonsillitis, prescribed some drugs, and then told Hattie that her daughter was disgracefully thin and under-nourished, and ought to be fed better. Hattie did not volunteer any information about laxatives and enemas.

The doctor was a kind, personable young man who, for instance, called Sybil "honey" and "my big girl" and who let her look down his throat as a reward for letting him look down hers. She wanted desperately for him to take her home with him. She had fastened a loose cufflink for him and hoped wistfully that he might enjoy such services on a permanent basis. When he returned with the test results and his prescriptions, she couldn't keep from asking him if he would like to have a little girl, but instead of replying he said that he had good news for her, that she could go home. As she watched him retreat in his white coat, her disappointment was so intense that it was Vicky, rather than Sybil, who made the long ride home with Hattie.

For the next half-dozen years, life went on about the same except for the escape now offered by increasingly frequent blank spells. Hattie's treatment of Sybil ranged from incredible spoiling (at one time the child had *fifty* dolls) to incredible battering. Another contrast was between the puritanical attitude toward sex in the Dorsett home during the day and the "primal scene" to which the child was exposed in her parents' bedroom at night amid considerable steamy commotion. Additional treats for Sybil (rarely) and her surrogate personalities (usually) came in the form of Hattie's subtle sexual molestation of neighborhood children, her evening defecations on the property of various families by whom she felt threatened, and her shoplifting at the grocery—all in between claims of close association with God, including information about the terrible things that this spirit of wrath and spite would do to children who ever tattled on their parents or who didn't love their mothers.

Part of Sybil's psychological battering came from Hattie's constant criticism. If Sybil did something, it probably was done wrong; and if anything went wrong, it was probably because of Sybil. An incident in this connection, in 1927 when Sybil was four, subjected the harassed child to a traumatic experience that echoed down the corridors of her life for the next thirty years or more. Hattie had taken her to visit relatives. While the grownups chatted in the living room after dinner, Sybil and Lulu, her equally young cousin, busily washed dishes in the kitchen. Lulu had just finished washing a glass pickle dish. After holding it up and letting Sybil admire it as it glistened in the light, she suddenly and unaccountably threw it against the French doors that separated the kitchen from the dining room, shattering both the dish and one of the doors.

In the pandemonium that followed, Lulu declared flatly that Sybil had broken the dish. Hattie, far from defending her daughter, accused her of breaking the dish deliberately. Frustrated and enraged by the injustice, the daughter—Peggy Lou—ran to the window and begged to be let out, all the time vehemently protesting her innocence. Her protests were futile. She was told to sit in the corner. Humiliation, but no corporal punishment; as she well knew, that would come later.

The Great Depression that began to settle over the land in 1929 reduced the Dorsetts from affluence almost to destitution. They lost their home in Willow Corners and had to move into a one-room house five miles out of town. To Hattie this experience must have been one of unbearable humiliation. Perhaps for this reason, perhaps for another, she fell into a catatonic state. Utterly passive and helpless, she had to be fed and clothed and kept clean by Willard and Sybil. It was hard work, a further burden added to the daily chores required by their poverty, but to Sybil this was a glorious period during which her mother let her alone. It was only a brief interlude, however. The catatonia ended abruptly in a melodramatic scene, with Hattie suddenly appearing at the crest of a snow-covered hill and, with her hysterical laugh, sledding down into a furrow and almost breaking her leg. Not long thereafter, though quite incidentally, the family's fortunes improved. The Dorsetts returned to town, and gradually life settled back to what Sybil considered normal.

About the only bright spot in her life was her father's mother, Mary Dorsett, who lived in a large bedroom upstairs. Although she didn't know about Hattie's aberrant behavior and therefore couldn't protect Sybil from it, she did offer the child the refuge and comfort of genuine affection. When Sybil was nine, however, Grandmother Dorsett died. Like the young doctor's departure from her life, the death was more than the young girl could take. Her grief was sharpened by rather shabby treatment from her parents, who thoughtlessly left her in her room during the funeral service and let her be assigned to the wrong car for the trip to the cemetery. After the coffin had been lowered into the grave, she had to be restrained from jumping in with it. At that moment she dissociated. That in itself was not unusual, but this was no ordinary blank spell. It lasted almost two years.

When it started Sybil was in the third grade. One day when she was eleven she found herself in a class that was very familiar yet somehow strange. The last class day she remembered was the one just before her grandmother's death, and she was not aware of any lapse of time. Yet today the room was not the same, the teacher was not the same, and her fellow students, though immediately recognizable, seemed bigger and were dressed differently. Indeed, she herself felt bigger, and she was wearing a dress that she had never seen before. At home she found many strange things, too—including the delightful surprise of having her own bedroom upstairs. She was afraid, of course, to confide in anyone about this experience. She kept it bottled up, and as time passed she adjusted well enough to keep anyone from suspecting her secret. She even managed to catch up on her fifth-grade classwork sufficiently to squeak through her quizzes and exams (her 170 IQ was a great blessing). Her greatest weakness was multiplication, which she had never been taught, but Vicky and Peggy Lou, who had, often emerged to help her through the really tight places.

And so she managed to live precariously with her other selves during the next ten years or so, through high school and even well into college. It was, however, a continual, nerve-wracking struggle, this never knowing when the next blank spell might arrive, how long it might last, or what fumbling, embarrassing explanations it might require of her. In June, 1945, at the end of her freshman year, the college administrators urgently recommended that she not return until she had received some psychiatric attention and her nerves were settled enough for her to resume her studies without further ruining her health. Her weight, for example, was down to 79 pounds.

At home she was as lonely as ever, although Hattie insisted on her company almost every moment of every day. This insistence proved fortunate, for otherwise Sybil might never have summoned up enough courage to visit a doctor on her own initiative. Shortly after Sybil's return, Hattie had an appointment in Omaha with her doctor and took her daughter along. As she sat in the waiting room, Sybil hoped desperately that the doctor would take some interest in her without her having to ask him (such was the depth of her diffidence). The possibility was remote, but perhaps her hope was intense enough to get a message through to the doctor.

When he appeared with Hattie in the waiting room, he asked Sybil if he could see her for a moment—alone. In his office he remarked on how unwell she looked and asked if there might be any way in which he could be of help. She answered with the truth, though by no means all the truth: she had been so nervous at college that she was told to seek psychiatric help. Well then, he responded matter-of-factly, if you like, I'll arrange an appointment with Dr. Cornelia Wilbur. She's right here in Omaha, and she works well with younger patients.

Sybil gratefully agreed. Her relief was almost physical. The doctor's reaction had been reassuringly casual, without a trace of surprise or disapproval. It had all been so easy.

And so it was with Dr. Wilbur about a week later. She listened to Sybil's story intently but calmly, without expressing anything even faintly resembling a judgment. All her life Sybil had been subjected to the Willow Corners brand of gratuitous criticism almost every time she opened her mouth, and now here she was, telling things about herself that she had never told anyone (but still nothing about her blank spells), without being interrupted, without a hint of censure. She had always feared that there was something radically wrong with her, and here was the doctor saying that her condition wasn't all that serious and that she could be helped. Not that the doctor was making light of the situation: after a few visits, she suggested that she arrange to have Sybil spend a little time in a local psychiatric hospital.

The suggestion created some consternation in the Dorsett household, a bastion of dim views on the subject of psychiatry in general and Dr. Wilbur in particular, since the woman smoked and probably even drank. After much discussion between themselves and their narrow but not unregenerate pastor, the Dorsetts ostensibly agreed. Meanwhile, however, Sybil had fallen prey to pneumonia and was unable to go to the hospital on the day scheduled. Hattie agreed to phone Dr. Wilbur and arrange a postponement. As Sybil listened from her bed, she made the phone call to all appearances, but she kept her finger on the cradle button to prevent the connection. It was not until three years later, with death approaching, that she told Sybil what she had done.

As might be expected, Sybil's bout with pneumonia was a long one. When she finally was well enough to call Dr. Wilbur, she discovered that the psychiatrist had left Omaha for New York to study, and then practice, psychoanalysis. Despite her disappointment she felt so encouraged by her few visits with the doctor that she decided to go back to college. This time she stayed, the only interruption being a mid-1948 trip to the Dorsetts' new home in Kansas City to nurse Hattie during the couple of months before her death. She received her bachelor's degree in June, 1949.

Over the next five years she kept house for her father, taught school, worked as an occupational therapist, and saved her money for a move to New York. She had two reasons for wanting to move to New York: to take graduate courses at Columbia University and to reestablish contact with Dr. Wilbur. She was still having her blank spells.

She made the move in September, 1954. After enrolling at the university, she phoned for an appointment with Dr. Wilbur, which she kept a few days later. The doctor readily understood her explanation of her failure to show up at the hospital nine years before, including the story of Hattie's deception, and they agreed to resume the sessions, especially now that the doctor was an analyst. This was to be the first of more than 2,300 sessions, stretched out over the next eleven years.

Sybil still couldn't bring herself to reveal her secret, much as other women have been reluctant to tell a doctor about a lump in the breast. She not only feared the implications, but she also dreaded disapproval, perhaps abandonment, by the doctor. Her unwillingness, however, was not entirely shared by the other personalities, and within a few months the doctor knew more about her problem then she did herself.

During a session late in December, 1954, the doctor watched in some astonishment as Sybil, during a tense discussion of some letters she had with her, suddenly tore them into shreds, hurled them into a wastebasket, and, running to a window, beat against it with her fist until she cracked the windowpane. Rushing over to her, the doctor brought her back to a chair, calming her with the most soothing words she could muster up for the occasion. She examined the offending hand and was relieved to see that it hadn't been cut, although a bruise was beginning to show.

Her concern over the hand impressed Peggy Lou (for that's who it was). In Willow Corners the chief concern would have been over the windowpane and the imperatives of punishment, but in this office the authority figure obviously was more interested in the bruised hand than in the broken pane. Indeed, the broken window didn't seem to bother her at all—the handyman could easily repair it, she explained. As for punishment, it clearly hadn't entered her mind.

Peggy Lou relaxed a bit and began to talk. The doctor also relaxed and began to listen. What she heard was puzzling. This was a much different person from the constrained Sybil Dorsett she knew—much more energetic in speech and gesture, much more open and forceful, much less inhibited, and surprisingly less careful about her diction. She also seemed younger, less mature. Finally the doctor, who until now had only done a little academic reading on the subject of multiple personality, bit the bullet and asked the girl who she was.

Peggy Lou Baldwin, the girl replied, surprised that the doctor hadn't been struck immediately by the imagined difference in appearance. She lived with Sybil, she reported, but her home was in Willow Corners. She liked to paint and sketch in charcoal, although she was not so talented as Sybil. The doctor asked if Hattie was her mother. The question seemed to terrify her. No, no, she protested—and suddenly Sybil was back, sitting quietly and rather primly in her chair.

She immediately recognized that the doctor must suspect her secret. Painfully embarrassed, she acknowledged that she must have broken the windowpane and offered to pay for the damage. The doctor tried to put her at ease, explaining that she had experienced what psychiatrists call a fugue. The fact that there was a name for it showed that it was not alarmingly unusual. And it was treatable. Sybil relaxed considerably. So much for now, thought the doctor; this obviously was no time to broach the subject of Peggy Lou.

She was still avoiding the subject in March, 1955, when she met Victoria Antoinette Scharleau. Unlike Peggy Lou, Vicky did not emerge in the middle of an interview. When the doctor opened her office door there was Vicky sitting in the waiting room, reading a copy of *The New Yorker*. She smiled at the doctor cheerily, entering the office with a grace totally uncharacteristic of either Peggy Lou or Sybil. Sybil wasn't feeling well this morning, Vicky explained, and so she decided to come instead. And who, asked the doctor warily, are you? Vicky apologized for not introducing herself, and immediately did so.

She talked very easily with the doctor, telling her about her family in Paris, her omniscience regarding Sybil and the other personalities. Oh, yes, she revealed, there were quite a few others. Stunned, the doctor asked how much Sybil knew about them. Not a thing, Vicky answered—to her we are just blank spells. There was Peggy Ann, for instance—but the doctor decided against a full litany in the few moments left of their hour. Instead, she asked Vicky to let them all know that they would be welcome in her office. Vicky agreed, for she was in a hurry to be on her way: she had an appointment to meet a friend for a spot of lunch and esthetic escape at the Metropolitan Museum of Art.

Over the next five years Dr. Wilbur got to know the various personalities as they took advantage of her invitation. They were, she found, quite a mixed bag, especially if one included their own perceptions of themselves. They ranged in age from near infancy to adulthood. Although they all were tainted and troubled by a strain of Willow Corners morality, a few were less affected than the others, and each seemed to have his or her own philosophy of life. Most were artists, of varying talents, but only one could play a musical instrument (Vanessa played the piano). Vicky had told the doctor in an early interview that all the personalities, including Sybil, were neurotic, but that she, Vicky, was not. The more the doctor got to know of Vicky and the others, the more she was inclined to agree, despite Vicky's delusions about her rather hifalutin relatives. As early as 1955, in fact, she asked Vicky for help in getting the various personalities to cooperate in the healing process.

Vicky agreed to do so, but the promise proved easier to make than to keep. Several of the personalities could be quite obstreperous at times (especially the Peggys), and Vicky was naturally sympathetic with their desire to be free of the tensely inhibited Sybil every so often. As a result, Sybil continued to dissociate repeatedly. Peggy Lou got her into some difficulty by trying to break into a car, which she mistook for her father's. Mary almost bought a house in her name. The two boys built a partition in the apartment she shared with another girl. Peggy Lou broke some $2,000 worth of glass bricabrac in various Fifth Avenue shops in a single year, all paid for of course by Sybil. And on January 7, 1958, Sybil found herself standing in front of a hotel in Philadelphia and looking at a newspaper with that date on it—and realizing that the last thing she remembered was being in class in New York on January 2 and hearing some glass break in the hall or the lab. On this and a few similar trips (including one to San Francisco), Peggy Lou had a ball.

After the return from Philadelphia of Sybil & Co., Dr. Wilbur interviewed Peggy Lou, and her inseparable companion Peggy Ann, about the trip and, with their permission, recorded their account of it. She had informed Sybil of the other personalities' existence three years before, but now, with an extended taped account of a dissociation, she could offer something to back up her story.

That story troubled Sybil deeply, creating a serious conflict between her abiding trust in Dr. Wilbur's honesty and her terrified unwillingness to accept the idea of "other selves." Now she almost fiercely resisted the doctor's urging that she listen to the tape. The ultimate goal of her treatment, the doctor explained, was to integrate all the personalities into one, and it seemed just about as far away now as it had three years ago. But Sybil's listening to the tape, and thus getting to know a couple of the other personalities and sharing their memories, could be a first step toward integration. The only alternative would be no progress whatsoever.

Sybil finally agreed, perhaps because of the irresistible logic of the doctor's argument, but more probably because her fear of alienating the doctor with a flat, unreasoning refusal was greater than her fear of the tape. Indeed, the first few feet of the tape sent her into a fit of terror, for the voice she heard was her mother's. The doctor had to stop the recorder and spend some considerable time convincing her that the voice was Peggy Lou's, for whatever reassurance that fact might offer. Eventually, with much backing and filling, Sybil did listen to the entire tape.

It was a sobering experience. But perhaps the last thing Sybil needed was a sobering experience. Although it may well have provided some hidden long-term benefits, the results over the next few months were anything but encouraging. Sybil continued to dissociate, and in the fall of 1958 she even attempted suicide (an attempt foiled by Vicky). Whether the attempt was really a determined effort may have been questionable, but a suicide attempt of any kind is not a source of comfort to a patient's psychiatrist. Up to this point Dr. Wilbur had felt that analysis would be the most gentle and ultimately most effective type of therapy. But now she began considering alternatives. There were three that might be worth trying, and in this order: electric shock, sodium pentothal, and hypnosis.

The electric shock treatments were futile and therefore few. Sodium pentothal, however, had a marked effect. For a day or so after each shot Sybil was in a state of blissful euphoria such as she had never known before. Further, the drug brought on some signs of integration: she could remember some of the things that had happened during a few of her blank spells. But by early 1959 it was clear that she was becoming psychologically addicted. The others, who had to some extent shared her euphoria, were now also to some extent sharing her growing addiction. The doctor was forced to call a halt.

The response was immediate: a kind of psychological turmoil among all concerned. Only Vicky expressed any sympathy with the doctor's concern over addiction. As a result, the pace of Sybil's improvement became glacial. Often she seemed to lose more ground than she could ever regain. By the fall of 1959, the doctor was ready for the last resort. Long before, she had promised Sybil that she would not hypnotize her. Now she asked to be released from that promise. When she had made it, she explained, she had not even suspected the kinds of problems that she was destined to encounter. She had read accounts of other cases of multiple personality—Christine Beauchamp, Eve White, *et al.*—and she was struck by the evident effectiveness of hypnosis. This seemed to confirm her own strong opinion that the multiple-personality syndrome was a form of hysteria, not of psychosis, since hysterics are characteristically susceptible to hypnotic suggestion. After listening to the arguments, Sybil consented, perhaps more in resignation than in agreement.

Under hypnosis the various personalities were much more accessible to the doctor, who now had to put this opportunity to good use. It occurred to her that a major obstacle to integration was the broad range of ages, or levels of maturity, exhibited by the personalities. How, for example, could Ruthie, who talked and behaved like a two-year-old, be successfully integrated with Vicky, who talked and behaved like (to use her term) a *femme du monde* in her twenties? Or, indeed, with Sybil herself? A first step, thought the doctor, might be to induce them all to grow up through hypnotic suggestion. At least it was worth trying.

She started with Ruthie, naturally enough. With Sybil in hypnotic trance, she called Ruthie out and asked her if she'd like to be three. Ruthie said she would, especially since she could then color with crayons. The doctor aged her the additional year through hypnotic suggestion, gave her a couple of months to enjoy being three, and then asked her if she'd like to be six. Yes, said Ruthie. And would you like to continue growing older? Oh, yes, replied Ruthie—she wanted to do all the things that the others could do. Soon she was six—with prospects.

Using variations of this technique with all the surrogate personalities—sometimes in what must be called group-therapy sessions for want of a better term—Dr. Wilbur slowly, patiently encouraged the growth process in each. By early April, 1960, they were all eighteen or older, and the doctor decided to take the final plunge. On April 21 she induced them all to consider themselves 37 years and 3 months old, which was Sybil's age. The immediate results were spectacular. On the following day Sybil, under hypnosis, met Ruthie and Vicky, and at least ostensibly the three of them integrated on the spot. This session marked the first time that Sybil had "met" any of the others, as well as providing the first positive signs of integration. The doctor's spirits rose considerably.

Sybil's pattern of progress and relapse continued. That summer Peggy Lou joined Vicky and Ruthie in Sybil, but only weeks later Sybil was in a state of almost suicidal depression. In January, 1962, in a very emotional interview, Sybil finally admitted her hatred of Hattie to the doctor and to herself. This was an aid to integration, which neverthe-

less proceeded in fits and starts, with the remaining personalities anxiously reluctant to participate in what they viewed as their gradual de-
mise. Happiness is integration, the doctor kept telling them, but it was
a proposition that they found hard to accept.

Sybil had been too sick to continue in school, but in August, 1964,
she managed to get and keep a job as a receptionist at a large hotel.
Here she met Ramon Allegre, from Colombia. He asked for a date, and
she consented. Later he asked for something more, and she refused. In
October he proposed marriage—he was a widower, and his children
needed Sybil as a mother as much as he wanted her as a wife. Sybil
found both aspects of his proposal attractive, but she was much too
uncertain of her condition to accept. Unfortunately, Dr. Wilbur was in
Europe at the time, and Sybil had no one to go to for advice. And so
Ramon, puzzled and hurt by her rejection, departed from her life as
abruptly as he had entered it.

Sybil was disconsolate, but she didn't go to pieces. When the doctor returned soon thereafter, Sybil realized that she had an unbroken
memory of the three months since the doctor's departure. In all that
time there had not been a single dissociation. And indeed this was the
beginning of the end. Although other personalities were still in the
wings, they were weakening, and they could emerge on stage now only
under hypnosis.

The climax (as it proved later) came in June, 1965. One evening,
at home in her apartment, Sybil had a sudden and severe gastrointes-
tinal attack which triggered a kind of seizure. Luckily, she managed to
telephone her new friend Flora Rheta Schreiber, who rushed to her
apartment and found her lying exhausted on the floor but proud that
she had been herself, her fully conscious self, through the whole experience. It was only after the doctor arrived, on a call from Flora, that
Sybil experienced her last dissociation. This time it was the nameless
blonde teenager, who rather vaguely identified herself in strangely ca-
denced prose and then reassured Flora and the doctor that she had no
intention of interfering with Sybil's recovery.

She was as good as her word. By mid-July Sybil felt well enough
to tell the doctor, for the first time and with unprecedented confidence, that she was sure that she had dissociated for the last time. In a
series of "test" interviews the doctor found that her patient indeed gave
every indication of being one. The other personalities, questioned
under hypnosis, proved to have not a single memory that Sybil didn't
have too. The memory bank was finally complete, and all in one place.

In September, 1965, the doctor made an entry in her office diary, "All personalities one."

The next month Sybil left New York for Pennsylvania, where she had been engaged by a hospital to work as an occupational therapist with emotionally disturbed children. As she had assured the doctor, she never did dissociate again.

Jonah, 1974

After a hundred years and about the same number of reported multiple-personality cases, Jonah was the first subject to undergo thorough objective testing. Eve White, Eve Black and Jane had been tested intermittently (and sometimes revealingly), but Jonah's testing was concentrated and comprehensive: besides a general physical and an intensive neurological examination, a battery of tests were administered to determine, so far as possible, the learning ability, memory, and personality characteristics of each of the personalities.*

The testing has been fully reported by psychiatrists of the University of Kentucky Medical School in the April, 1972, *Archives of General Psychiatry* and in *The International Journal of Clinical and Experimental Psychosis* for 1974. Drs. Jeffrey Brandsma and Arnold Ludwig seem to have been chief spokesmen for the group, which also included Dr. Cornelia Wilbur, who had encountered half a dozen cases of multiple personality after her treatment of Sybil Dorsett.

During about the first twenty years of his life Jonah behaved normally, or at least with enough restraint to avoid widespread comment. But one day in 1964, while serving as a G.I. Joe in Germany, he was told that a good friend had died in action in Vietnam. Evidently he suffered a blackout, during which he started a roaring fire in the company garbage pit. The next year he himself saw his first action in Vietnam, and he reacted by indiscriminately firing his rifle all about him until he

---

*The testing included electroencephalography, Rorschach, Visual Evoked Response, Finger Tapper Test and Roughness Discrimination, Paired-Words and Emotionally Laden Words tasks, Draw Self tasks, Wechsler Adult Intelligence Scale, Kent Series of Emergency Scales, Shipley Institute of Living Scale, Associate Learning and Logical Memory subtests from the Wechsler Memory Scale (Forms I and II), Minnesota Multiphasic Personality Inventory, and Adjective Check List.

135

was subdued by his buddies in panicky self-defense. Since his company commander took a dim view of this behavior, he was sent to a hospital for a psychiatric check. This led to a long series of psychiatric examinations which culminated in a medical discharge.

Back in the States, he enlisted in the Job Corps in 1966 and was sent to New England. One morning he woke up unaccountably drenched to the skin. During the night, his comrades informed him, he had taken an unscheduled dip in the Atlantic Ocean. He was headed for an island lighthouse when he was picked up some 500 yards from shore. On another morning some months later he awakened in a jail cell; in a bar the night before, he was told, he had assaulted and battered a couple to settle an argument. In 1968 he was caught by the police at a river bank, where he was busily engaged in drowning his latest adversary, an operation that luckily proved unsuccessful. In each of these episodes he suffered a memory blackout; over the years he had had many other blackouts for which he could offer no explanation, for in these cases there was no one to tell him later what had happened.

In the three weeks preceding his first admission to the Medical School in 1970, during blackouts he had twice beaten his wife, threatened her with a knife, and thrown her out of the house along with their three-year-old daughter. When his wife later described the incidents to him, she told him that he had called himself Usoffa Abdulla, son of Omega. This dismaying news was augmented shortly thereafter by another blackout adventure involving a stabbing and a police chase. Thoroughly frightened, Jonah sought help and was referred to the Medical School, where he was placed in the care of Dr. Wilbur.

He had these damn blackouts, he told the doctor, during which he did strange and sometimes terrible things that he never remembered afterward. A blackout usually was preceded by a sharp headache that started as a circlet of pain and then spread over his head. After emerging from the blackout he would no longer be in pain and would even feel quite comfortable. These and other biographical details were confirmed by his wife and friends and by Army and other records—as well as by incidents in the ward over the next several days. He did indeed have frequent blackouts during which he behaved very differently and after which he denied remembering anything that had occurred. Luckily he did not go berserk in any of these incidents, but as they continued over the next few weeks the psychiatrists grew ever more impressed with the signs of separate, discrete personalities, each exhibiting his own individual traits. Since hypnosis had proved a useful therapeutic tool in similar cases, the doctors decided to give it a try. It proved to be very effective, at least on the surface. Some eight weeks after his admission Jonah seemed well enough integrated to be discharged. In releasing him the doctors had some serious misgivings, but they also had the problem of balancing his needs and condition against those of other patients requiring their time and attention.

The cure did not last. During the following nine months Jonah dissociated often, on two occasions waking up to find himself in jail. The incident that really blew him apart again, it seems, concerned a newly acquired doxy: as he approached her place one night he saw a man leaving and then found her in the apartment naked. The violence that ensued soon led to his readmission to the Medical School.

This time it was decided to use hypnosis, at least at first, for interviewing the various personalities under more controlled conditions than Jonah himself could provide. He went into trances quickly and easily, and the personalities would usually emerge on call most obligingly. This procedure, with some backing and filling and considerable cross-checking, brought to light four distinct personalities. Jonah was considered the primary one not only by the doctors but also by the three other personalities, who all knew him but whom he did not know. Not surprisingly, he was also the diffident one—withdrawn, timid, reticent, rather lethargic, and very proper in his views and conduct. He was generally unresponsive in interviews, and his emotional reactions seemed superficial.

Sammy was the unflappable one, a man of dispassionate intellect. His story was that he had first arrived on deck after a bloody fight between the parents. Upon their return home—the stepfather from the hospital and the mother from jail—Sammy imperiously confronted them with a criticism of their unconscionable behavior, warning them that their children should never again be exposed to such a scene. And evidently they never were.

Sammy also was the ever-conscious one, aware of what was going on regardless of who might be on deck, and in general privy to Jonah's consciousness. For this reason, and in view of his mental versatility and agility, he felt obliged to help Jonah out of his perennial succession of scrapes. Always available for legal counsel, he may have been one reason why Jonah hadn't been put away permanently years before.

King Young was the self-appointed Casanova, ever ready to play Cyrano to Jonah's Christian. He was generally amiable but was especially engaging when female doctors or attendants were present. The reason for his first emergence, he said, was that Jonah, when about seven, wore girl's clothes around the house at his mother's urging. When he began having trouble with sexual identification at school, King Young felt impelled to take over and straighten things out. He had been performing this chore ever since, and loving it.

While King Young felt only casually acquainted with Jonah and knew of the other personalities only through hearsay, Usoffa Abdulla, son of the god Omega, felt that he knew Jonah intimately. He knew of the others also only through hearsay, and he couldn't have cared less. Remote, bellicose, irascible, taciturn, sardonic, Usoffa emerged whenever Jonah was threatened with violence and subsided when the threat was over. Being very serious about this role of defender, he himself was often grimly threatening in demeanor, and the doctors found him a rather frightening individual to interview. He had emerged for the first time one day when Jonah, then about ten, fainted during a vicious attack by some white roughnecks after school (Jonah was black). Abdulla, a real gut fighter, got up and nearly murdered a couple of the attackers, finally driving them off. From then on he accepted intimidation and physical violence as his natural role. The doctors were relieved to learn that a fifth personality, who promised to be much more formidable than Usoffa, was still undeveloped and would not be available for interviewing.

The extensive testing of these four personalities, conducted by Dr. Brandsma, took about a week. In general—besides ruling out any serious possibility of fakery—the results revealed the same sets of traits that the various personalities had exhibited during the interviews, but only in emotional areas. Abdulla did show up as contentious and hostile, for instance, and King Young was revealed as girl crazy (e.g., his self-portraits regularly included a female companion). But the differences were negligible in nonemotional areas: all the personalities had about the same rather low IQ, for example, including Sammy the Brain. As for memory, none of the four could remember what had happened when anyone else was on deck, with one exception: the three secondary personalities could remember, more or less, what had happened when Jonah was on deck. Yet in the Emotionally Laden Words tasks, Jonah reacted strongly to all *their* significant words, but they each reacted only to their own. And Abdulla was found to have some degree of anesthesia in certain areas of his body, a happy abnormality for someone fond of violence.

Given the correlation in the results of interviewing and testing, the researchers concluded that, in areas of emotional significance, each personality was remarkably distinct and substantially sealed off from the others. The evidence, they felt, supported their argument that "the category of multiple personality be viewed as a unique entity." In this connection it may be significant that the *Index Medicus* recently added "Multiple Personalities" to the list of reference subject headings. In a sense, perhaps, Mary Reynolds is finally coming into her own.

After the first week of testing, another two weeks were devoted to therapy. In a series of bargaining sessions conducted under hypnosis, all the personalities promised to cooperate in an effort at integration into a combined, fifth personality to be named Jusky (a kind of acronym of their four names). Some subsequent testing of Jusky indicated that by and large he shared the characteristics of all four personalities, but with extremes largely eliminated. There was some suggestion of impulsiveness and vagrant cerebration, but not enough to cause alarm. He was discharged with the understanding that he would come in for a checkup at least once a month, an agreement that, at the time when the final report was submitted for publication, he was still honoring. Despite the appearance of Sammy on a couple of occasions when anxiety became intolerable, he generally seemed to be (almost literally) holding together.

As for the emergence of Sammy on occasion, this cannot be automatically deplored as undesirable. As many of the cases described here imply, some of us might find a Sammy (though perhaps not an Abdulla) very helpful now and then in getting us over the humps. As these authors and others have suggested, every one of us may have a secondary personality or two lurking beneath our calm exterior.

Henry Hawksworth, 1977

It was another case of child abuse. In 1936 Henry Hawksworth was barely three years old, but he had already received many severe beatings from his macho-oriented father, who also forced his son to stand under a numbingly cold shower after each beating in the finest of sadistic drill-instructor traditions. Further, the obsessive disciplinarian was inconsistent, at different times punishing and praising his son for the same kinds of behavior, so that the child was utterly frustrated in his efforts to avoid the pain of the beatings and the terror of the ice-cold showers. Like most children, especially lonely children, he sought refuge in his imagination, inventing playmates for distraction and consolation. Unlike most other children, he fell asleep one afternoon and stayed asleep for the next forty years, allowing his imaginary companions to take over his life.

On the preceding evening a spark from the fireplace at home had set his pajamas on fire. Although his father had quickly smothered the flames and put the unhurt boy to bed with rare solicitude, Henry woke the next morning sharply fearful of the punishment he might receive if catching on fire proved to be a bad thing to do. The more he thought about it that morning, as he contemplated the dreaded penalty that the evening might bring, the more tense he grew. By afternoon nap time he was "beside himself" more literally than that phrase ordinarily implies. As Henry fell asleep he came apart. For the next forty years Dana, Johnny, Peter and Phil—and, briefly near the end, Jerry—would come and go, weaving in and out of his life as they followed their very different inclinations.

Dana was the primary of these personalities, an amiable if rather stolid fellow of great practical intelligence. As an adult he was the breadwinner, functioning very successfully as a salesman and sales executive. Yet during the forty years he was fired from (or in a few cases quit) a total of 31 jobs because of Johnny's outrageously antisocial behavior. Johnny was his, or Henry's, self-disgust distilled in his own flesh and blood. Although Dana did not know about Johnny (he knew only that he had mysterious lapses), Johnny knew and deeply hated "that chickenshit Dana." This hostile, misanthropic alter-ego was erratic, irresponsible, irascible, uninhibited and utterly dedicated to the pleasures of brawl, bar and bed. The fact that he lost Dana's jobs, as well as earning him an impressive record of citations for drunk and reckless driving and leaving him in embarrassing and often painful predicaments, simply added to his pleasure. Any success or satisfaction that Dana might achieve invariably goaded Johnny into coming out, taking control, and wreaking gleeful havoc. He fought dirty, talked dirty, thought dirty, and drove automobiles like a kamikaze stuntman. He liked nothing better than to leave the puzzled Dana in jail on a drunk-driving charge, in bed with a whore, in a strange town without any money after a three-day lapse, and so on. Sometimes he would put out his cigarette on his own arm before departing, leaving Dana to deal with the pain.

This Mr. Hyde was outnumbered by three Dr. Jekylls. Besides Dana, there were Peter and Phil. Peter was Johnny's opposite—peaceful, thoughtful, unsophisticated and childlike yet capable of writing publishable poetry. Phil, who appeared very seldom except near the end of the forty-year period, embodied the instinct for self-preservation, stepping in to protect Dana whenever he could. But the vigorous, aggressive Johnny, although outnumbered by these benign personalities, was more than a match for them. While he seemed able to come and go almost at will, they generally could emerge only with difficulty. On occasion they had to resort to forcing their advice into Dana's consciousness, or semiconsciousness. In these rare cases he would hear voices, indistinctly but unmistakably. Although he might follow the advice, the experience frightened him. The addition of these voices to his frequent attacks of amnesia naturally made him wonder about his sanity. As with most of us, however, this was not the sort of question that invited contemplation or action. How often have we resisted going to a doctor for fear of what he or she might say?

Dana could hardly be blamed for having such an attitude. During his junior year in high school, when Johnny and sometimes even Peter were making his life unbearable and his grades atrocious, and when the principal suggested to his father that the boy needed psychological help, Dana was agreeable. His father, however, would have no truck with psychiatry, sending his son instead to the family doctor. This physician evidently considered his religious fundamentalism an adequate substitute for medical competence. When his examination revealed no obvious physical problem, he informed Dana that his problem was sin and that the devil had to be driven out of him. To this end he dispatched the boy to visit a couple of preachers who nearly asphyxiated him with their irrelevant zealotry. He did not return for a second visit.

Many years later, thinking his problem might be alcohol (he suspected that he got roaring drunk during many of his lapses), he sought help in Alcoholics Anonymous. But alcohol was not his problem, although he spent the next 18 months going to the meetings. At this point Johnny, having had it up to here with put-downs of his precious booze, emerged to attend a meeting at which he taunted the group with being "drinking failures" and from which, after leaving behind two bottles of whiskey to tempt them, he flew to Reno for a riotous week. Dana awoke one morning in a Reno hotel room to find himself in bed with a hangover and some woman's underthings and cosmetics in the bathroom. He returned to his home in California but never again to Alcoholics Anonymous.

Incidents like this, of course, contributed nothing to a happy home life. In the mid-fifties, not long after his discharge from a rather chaotic hitch in the Marine Corps, he had married his wife Ann largely through the machinations of the romantic Peter. The couple had three children, and the family was supported erratically but often opulently by Dana's impressive string of intermittent business successes. Despite her genuine love for Dana, Ann was sorely tried by his unexplained (or inadequately explained) absences and occasionally bizarre conduct. And Dana, despite his genuine love for Ann, could not bring himself to reveal his anxiety over his mental condition. The strain on the marriage, and on him, grew ever worse. Although a brief visit with a Navy psychiatrist during his service years had proved futile, he decided to try again. This time the diagnosis was that he was a manic-depressive. For some months thereafter he took his prescribed amphetamines and tranquilizers, to no avail. The lapses continued as before.

Since he had lost so many jobs in California, he and Ann decided, desperately, to try their luck in another state. They packed up and moved to Salt Lake City. But history simply repeated itself. He was hired as a clerk in a 7-11 store and during the next months was successively promoted, eventually to the position of assistant district manager responsible for a dozen stores. But then Johnny emerged, used

Dana's key to steal $1,200 from a store's safe in the early morning hours, and went on a 24-hour spree. On the following morning Dana was arrested and charged with grand larceny, with bail set at $5,000. Ann managed to raise $550 for a bondsman but, after Dana's release, tearfully announced that she was taking the children with her back to California, where they could live with her parents for a while. Dana, thus abandoned and charged with a crime he knew nothing about, was so thoroughly depressed that Phil took over, arranging a plea bargain, pleading guilty to a misdemeanor, and accepting a sentence of 90 days in jail, with bail reduced to $500.

Before he could begin serving the sentence, however, Johnny took control again and took off for a high-speed trip to Nevada. The state police who interrupted his 95-mile-an-hour flight, not knowing that he was a fugitive, simply gave him a speeding ticket and let him go his way. Three nights later, as Johnny was about to go to bed with an attractive and compliant young thing whom he had picked up in a bar, Phil forced his way into control again and began putting his clothes back on, calmly informing his startled companion that he had just recalled something that would require him to leave immediately. Back in a hotel in Salt Lake City, he left a note advising Dana to return to California in the morning, since he would not be extradited for a misdemeanor. Dana found the note when he awoke next morning (it was signed "Your Friend") and did indeed return to California.

There he managed to persuade Ann to reunite the family in the very real love that bound them together. But the effort was in vain. Johnny—and, increasingly now, Peter—would give him no peace. After his next loss of a job he turned in despair to their family doctor. The doctor, aware that Dana was unemployed, recommended the county hospital's free group-therapy program. Dana spent some time there, mostly following instructions to beat a pillow acting as a father surrogate, after which he departed with the conviction that the patients as a group were probably saner than the therapists. The frustrating lapses continued. And Ann left with the children for Canada.

But one day in March, 1975, hope appeared in the form of Dr. Ralph Allison, a psychiatrist acquainted with the phenomena of multiple personality. Dana, having read about the recently discovered calming effects of lithium treatments, had called Allison's office in the hope of investigating that possibility. On his first visit he failed to mention his lapses, and the doctor tentatively prescribed lithium, which had no perceptible effect over the next few days. On his second visit the doctor asked him, under hypnosis, why he got drunk, and upon awakening Dana remarked that he didn't drink, although Johnny did. He did not know why he had said such a thing, nor did he know who this Johnny might be. But the doctor seized on the clue and, after some more questioning, offered the possible diagnosis of multiple personality.

Dana in his turn seized on the possibility. For the first time in his life he had some hope that he might have an identifiable illness, one which might be adequately diagnosed and perhaps even cured. He was so excited by the thought that he phoned Ann in Canada. As she listened to him she recognized how much of his behavior throughout their marriage could be explained by this hypothesis, and she began to share his excitement. Once again love conquered all, and she and the children returned to California.

Over the next several months and in many sessions with Dr. Allison (attended by a fascinated and sympathetic Ann), and with the help of a Polaroid camera with which the doctor took snapshots of the various personalities for Dana's startled post-hypnotic viewing, the patient started on the road to reintegration. The lithium was more helpful now, guarding Dana against extreme moods in which Johnny would find it easy to emerge. By means of hypnosis and automatic writing the doctor helped Dana to search through the past, calling out the other personalities for information on incidents that Dana had never known about. As the sessions continued, Dana seemed to be improving, but it was not until November that he first mentioned Henry. In response to Dr. Allison's question, he explained that Henry Dana Hawksworth was his full name. But the revelation seemed to have no particular significance, and neither he nor the doctor pursued it.

In March, 1976, Johnny erupted again, furiously breaking things up in a store where Dana worked and sticking him with a serious drunk-driving charge. After Ann had disconsolately bailed him out, Dana was so depressed that he came close to suicide, from which Phil narrowly rescued him. He continued his therapy with Dr. Allison, however, despite frightening misgivings. Actually the healing process was further along than he realized. With much encouragement from Jerry, he managed to eradicate Johnny from his life, and after this he and Phil and Peter, as well as Jerry, were quite willing to withdraw permanently in favor of Henry. Henry now had to acquaint himself with himself, with his wife and children, with the doctor, and with his employer, who on being informed of his illness had offered to give him his old job back. But the learning process was astonishingly and gratifyingly swift, and by the end of May Henry finally seemed to be in full control.

The trial on the drunk-driving charge was held in June. Henry's defense was based on his multiple-personality syndrome, maintaining his innocence on the grounds, in effect, that the guilty party, Johnny, no longer existed. Dr. Allison, as chief defense witness, used hypnosis to reveal the various personalities to the judge, who found the demonstration so persuasive that he had arrived at a decision even before the district attorney's final cross-examination. Since it could not be proved beyond reasonable doubt that Henry had been drunk when arrested, he must be declared not guilty. Charge dismissed.

Not long thereafter Henry, with the help of Ted Schwarz, a professional writer, began writing his unusual autobiography, published by Regnery in 1977 under the title *The Five of Me*. As he put it near the end of the book, his forty-year nightmare was finally over.

William Milligan, 1981

October, 1977, was an extraordinary month on the campus of Ohio State University. Three women had been reported as abducted from the area on three separate occasions and taken to a remote location, there to be robbed and raped. While the local media began running stories featuring "The Campus Rapist," harried police squads from Columbus and the university began running down leads. The evidence quickly focused on a prime suspect, an ex-convict living near the campus. After his arrest the evidence against him burgeoned: the women's credit cards found in his possession, identification through mug shots and in a lineup, fingerprints. Early in November a grand jury indicted him for kidnapping, robbery and rape. On the next day the prisoner, William Milligan, tried to commit suicide by hitting his head against the cement wall of his jail cell.

He could not remember committing the crimes. Or so he said, and Judy Stevenson, the lawyer appointed to his case by the public defender's office, believed him. She was struck, moreover, by how differently he behaved at different times. During the first several interviews with him she grew ever more aware that this case promised to go beyond the commonplace. Her client so often seemed confused and disoriented that she wondered about his competence to stand trial. And so, at her urging, a clinical psychologist was called in to examine him. The diagnosis: acute schizophrenia, with severe identity problems. Milligan reported regularly hearing voices ordering him to perform various actions and berating him roundly for any failures to obey. He believed the voices belonged to demonic persons inhabiting his body from time to time, alternating with other, benevolent persons who tried to protect him. The psychologist recommended that Milligan be sent to a hospital for additional examination and treatment as appropriate.

When the public defender's office requested a court order to carry out this recommendation, the judge agreed to the extent of directing

146

that Milligan undergo a series of interviews to be conducted at the jail by the forensic psychiatry unit of a Columbus mental health center. When the prisoner returned from this hearing to the jail, he was put in a strait jacket and confined to an infirmary cell because the sheriff's men remembered that, just before the hearing, he had managed to smash the toilet bowl in his cell and had tried to slash his wrists with a fragment of porcelain. But later, when they checked on him, they were astonished to find him sleeping peacefully with his head resting on the removed, and folded, jacket.

The interviews were conducted during February and early March, 1978, by a psychologist from the center. In the first, Milligan did not respond to the name of Billy but insisted that he was David, that Billy was asleep, and that he would not be awakened because Arthur would not permit it. When pressed for an explanation, he refused to give any more information because doing so would get him in dutch with "the others." Only eight years old, he was terrified when he realized that he had let Arthur's name slip out. Asked about "the others," he would say only that there were quite a lot of them and that he knew only some of them. He spoke and behaved like an eight-year-old despite his —Milligan's—six-foot height and 190 pounds. The psychologist had expected, on her arrival, to have a job with which she was well acquainted, that of unmasking a dissembler. But she had never seen a performance as convincing as this.

In the second interview David had been replaced by Christopher, a 13-year-old boy with a Cockney accent and a talent, he claimed, for playing the drums and the 'armonica. Unlike the timid, withdrawn David, he was outgoing and even cheery. He would not discuss the others, however; David had been a bad boy and had gotten into trouble, he explained, by telling "the secret," and he had no intention of following his example. Yet he did say that he was from England and, when asked whether he had any brothers or sisters, mentioned a Christene, aged three.

On her arrival for her third visit the psychologist immediately saw that she was confronting neither David nor Christopher but rather an insouciant, self-possessed someone else. This one turned out to be 16-year-old Tommy, who insisted that he had never seen her before and therefore refused to respond to any questions. After spending about a quarter of an hour in a futile effort to extract some information from this increasingly sullen teenager, she left the jail and returned to the health center, where she telephoned Judy Stevenson. Since she had promised David not to tell "the secret," she felt some moral obligation to maintain confidentiality; yet Stevenson obviously had some right to know, if she was to handle the defense. On the phone she asked Stevenson if she had ever read Flora Rheta Schreiber's book, *Sybil*. No. Then please get a copy, she urged, and read it.

Stevenson did so and got the point, but she was skeptical. She had observed that Milligan behaved strangely, she told the psychologist the next day, and that he often changed moods rapidly, but she had seen nothing as extreme as in the Sybil case. This reasonable but frustrating reaction gave the psychologist the incentive, in her next interview, to tell David, who happened to be "out" when she arrived, that she really must tell his lawyer, or their lawyer, the secret. David refused, excitedly and adamantly. She persisted. His eyes went blank for a moment. Then, in a tight-lipped British accent, sitting straight in his chair and glowering, he informed her that she must not break her promise to the boy. After taking a minute to recover, she suggested that they had not met before. He rather coldly identified himself as Arthur. Over the next quarter hour she argued valiantly for revealing the secret to the defense lawyer, but to no avail. Neither the lawyer nor anyone else, Arthur insisted, would believe it. In the end, after a moment of blank staring, he receded and was replaced by a congenial youth of 18 named Allen, who explained that it was he who had done most of the talking with Stevenson and, on occasion, her supervisor. He was usually given such assignments because he got along well with people. And indeed he was much friendlier than Arthur, yet quite as adamant when it came to revealing the secret.

The interview lengthened into hours as the psychologist pressed her case with the various personalities as they emerged and receded. Finally her persistence proved her to be the irresistible force against the not so immovable object. As the characters in the drama began weakening, she extracted a commitment from each to go along with telling the secret if all the others agreed. But she had to promise that it would go no further than Stevenson—who, when told of the arrangement, was surprised and a bit chagrined that she could not tell her supervisor. Nevertheless she eagerly accepted an invitation to attend the next interview.

At that meeting the two women were greeted by a 14-year-old named Danny, a talented painter who stayed out long enough to say that he did still lifes but never landscapes. When asked why no landscapes, he mumbled something about not liking the ground and about

somebody killing him if he explained why. With this mysterious remark he receded and was replaced by the congenial Allen. He recognized Stevenson at once, repeating his explanation that it was usually
he who had talked to her and her supervisor in the past. But, she remonstrated, he had answered to the name of Billy. Of course, he answered, since they had assumed he was Billy and he had no reason to
disabuse them. But Billy was almost always asleep. He, Allen, and the
others had to keep him asleep because of his suicidal impulses, although
he sometimes emerged despite their efforts. And indeed, later that day
Stevenson received a phone call at home reporting that her client had
again tried to commit suicide—or at least that was the construction put
upon his behavior—by hitting his head against the wall.

There now were two people convinced that this must be a genuine
case of multiple personalities. At the next interview they launched an
effort to get permission to let the supervisor in on the secret. It took
three days, but finally everyone agreed, and the supervisor was invited
to attend the next session. Militantly skeptical, he accepted the invitation as much out of curiosity as anything else. As the interview progressed, his curiosity soon got the better of his skepticism, and before
long he found himself quizzing the various personalities as though they
were indeed different persons. Tommy, he learned, in addition to being
the Houdini for whom strait jackets were such a minor inconvenience,
was also a competent electrician. Arthur was the intellectual, the articulate and knowledgeable sophisticate, a kind of superego who usually
was in control when conditions were calm. When there was trouble,
however, he turned control over to the formidable Ragen, a protective
strongman with a prodigious talent for expressing rage. Upon request
(the personalities were becoming more cooperative) Arthur receded in
favor of Ragen, who informed his inquisitors, in a low, vibrant voice
and with a heavy Slavic accent, that he recognized that the police had
incontrovertible evidence that he had committed the three robberies.
But not rape. He was no rapist.

A skeptical supervisor had joined the meeting expecting to spend
perhaps a quarter hour with the client. Five hours later a converted
supervisor left the meeting wondering aloud, to Stevenson, how they
could possibly persuade the prosecutor's office and the judge to give
the Milligan assemblage their serious consideration. A long discussion
produced an idea. Dr. George Harding, Jr., of the Harding Hospital,
was one of Ohio's most respected and conscientious psychiatrists, a
man whose testimony even prosecutors trusted in evaluating insanity

pleas. If they could persuade him to attend an interview, and if he accepted Milligan's cast of characters as multiple personalities—or at least accepted the possibility—he might be willing not only to throw his considerable weight in their direction but even to admit Milligan into his hospital for diagnosis and treatment. Since it was worth a try, the supervisor visited Harding, and tried. Harding, though very skeptical, consented to attend an interview.

Meanwhile the mental health center officials had arranged for Dr. Cornelia Wilbur, of *Sybil* fame, to examine the Milligan menage. A meeting was set up for March 12, with Wilbur leading the interviewing and with Harding, the two public defenders, and the chief prosecutor present, along with personnel from the mental health center. The experienced Wilbur proved a very forceful interviewer, insisting that she be allowed to talk with Billy, the core personality. After conversations with Danny, Arthur, Allen and Ragen, she succeeded in calling out a fearful, utterly confused Billy whose lifetime memory seemed to consist mostly of lapses. Although Billy had nothing conclusive to say, the next day Dr. Harding advised the judge that the prisoner was not competent to stand trial. He also agreed to accept Milligan for a three-month period of pretrial observation and treatment at Harding Hospital. The prosecutor, out of conviction laced with bewilderment, concurred, as did the judge.

Shortly before Milligan's transfer to the hospital on March 16, Stevenson had a call from the psychologist, who had continued interviewing him at the jail. Another personality had appeared, she reported, making ten in all by her count. This one was a 19-year-old woman who had allegedly replaced Ragen during the rapes—and who was, she had explained, a lesbian.

Milligan's three-month stay at Harding Hospital lengthened, with court permission, into almost seven months, from mid-March into October, as Dr. Harding and his staff helped their unusual patient to fuse pairs of similar personalities into single personalities, which could then be further paired and fused until all would fuse finally into Billy. Much of the therapy involved getting Billy to recall memories long buried in the others' minds, including the violent treatment and sexual abuse which he had allegedly received at the hands of his stepfather and which, as he recalled it, had precipitated his first dissociation at the age of eight. Among the memories was one that seemed to explain Danny's earlier remark about not painting landscapes because he didn't like the ground, as well as his fear of being killed. The stepfather, as he and now Billy remembered it, had threatened to kill him and bury his body in the barn, even digging a hole and interring the boy in it briefly as a foretaste. (All the allegations were later heatedly denied by the step-father.)

Early in October Dr. Harding reported to the court that William Milligan, although mentally ill and not responsible for his crimes of a year earlier, now had a sufficiently integrated personality to be declared competent to stand trial. The public defenders opted for an insanity plea, though recognizing that the multiple personality syndrome was considered a neurotic disorder, not a psychotic state. The judge, in a brief hearing, accepted the conclusion of the Harding report and set Milligan's trial for December 4. The prosecutors concurred in the multiple-personality aspect of the case but would not agree that Milligan was insane.

Back in jail again at first, and then in custody at a local psychiatric hospital, Billy was soon aware that his fusion, his integration, was precarious. Since his moustache had disappeared and he could not remember shaving it off, he knew that he was experiencing fugues. Vaguely he felt that Arthur and Ragen were waiting quietly in the wings, prepared to take over if necessary—especially if he went to prison, where only Ragen could defend him. His fusion held well enough, however, to get him through the trial and the attendant media publicity. At the trial he listened quietly, if often tearfully, while the public defenders presented depositions from his mother and brother confirming his lapses into trances, his varying behavior, and the indications of child abuse. He remained calm while the judge—the defense had prudently waived the right to a jury trial—found him not guilty by reason of insanity and remanded him, through the probate court, to the state mental health center in Athens, Ohio. He even talked quite lucidly, though briefly, to the reporters who lined his path from the courtroom to the van that was to take him to Athens. But the ride there was a rough one for him, and it was Danny, not Billy, who arrived at the mental health center.

Fortunately his chief therapist there was the medical director, Dr. David Caul, a psychiatrist recommended by Dr. Wilbur because he had some experience with "multiples." At the center, Dr. Caul encouraged visits from Billy's family and provided him with the necessary room and materials for painting to his heart's content. And Milligan, responding to this physician's skillful, cautious, solicitous treatment, not only uncovered 14 other, suppressed personalities but also fused all 24 into one of the 14 called The Teacher—a fusion triggered by his being shown a TV recording of Ragen testifying that The Teacher and Billy were one and the same. This personality turned out to be the original, genuine William Milligan in a final integration that at last gave every indication of being the real thing. In addition, when Milligan was bombarded with offers from publishers for his life story, Caul helped him select a trustworthy professional writer, an English professor from Ohio University in Athens, Daniel Keyes. The result was a detailed biography, *The Minds of Billy Milligan*, published by Random House in 1981.

Over the next two years, in hundreds of hours of interviews with Milligan the Teacher, his family, friends, lawyers, therapists, jailers and victims, Keyes pieced together Milligan's bizarre story. He got acquainted with the remaining personalities—Phil the hoodlum, Lee the comic, Steve the mimic, Bobby the dreamer, April the vixen and Shawn the deaf child, among others. He learned that Milligan had experienced his first dissociation as early as the age of three. Shortly after his natural father's suicide, in his loneliness Billy often became little Christene, who could play with his younger sister more comfortably than a boy could. Not long thereafter, to avoid the frightening noise of angry discipline, he sometimes became the deaf child Shawn—and then, to escape the pain of physical punishment, at home or at school, sometimes the lugubrious boy David. After such "becomings" Billy would come to and wonder why he was in another room, or why he had those red marks on his knuckles, or why his eyes were brimming with tears. But he was happy about not being yelled at any longer, or being spanked, or having his knuckles rapped.

Thus Billy was aware of losing patches of time. He assumed everybody did. (When he began to suspect otherwise later in life, his condition became "the secret.") His lapses were noticed by others, too, especially by members of his family, not of course as absences but as instances of moody, mercurial behavior. "That's not my Billy," his mother would say at times, more perceptively than she knew, "that's the *other* Billy." After her remarriage the boy's stepfather allegedly took Billy out to the farm, had him dig a hole, and buried him (now Danny) in it with a piece of pipe in his mouth for air to illustrate what would happen to him if he blabbed about any mistreatment. The child's moody, mercurial behavior did not thereafter improve.

It got him into continual trouble as he grew older, both in and out of school, so much so that his bewilderment and frustration over his lapses began turning at times to suicidal depression. On one occasion he stepped into the path of a moving automobile, which stopped before carrying out his ostensible purpose. Soon thereafter he was taken to a doctor, who diagnosed him as having "psychic trances"; his prognosis and treatment, if any, are not recorded. In March, 1970, when he was 14, he was committed to the children's section of the Columbus State Hospital. He stayed there only until June, when he was released at the request of his mother and to the considerable relief of the hospital staff.

One day in the fall, in his freshman year at high school, Billy was accosted in a corridor by a gaggle of sexually aggressive girls. He was a virgin, wasn't he, they taunted. Not knowing that Phil had recently been introduced to the coital exercise by a formidably alluring nymphet at a swimming party, Billy confessed his innocence. The maidens, their libidos whetted, intensified the teasing until they managed to force him into a girls' washroom, remove his trousers, and escape with their prize, leaving him on the floor clad only in shirt and shorts. Although he was soon rescued from this predicament by a teacher returning his trousers (Ragen had been immobilized by his refusal to strike a woman), Billy was so painfully ashamed—he could never face those girls again—that he climbed the stairs to the roof of the school building and, after leaving a note in one of his books that he just couldn't take it any more, started for the edge of the roof at a run. But he was stopped in time by Ragen. Shortly thereafter Arthur and Ragen had a serious discussion, agreeing that Billy would have to be put to sleep indefinitely for his own, and their own, safety. And so it would be for the next seven years.

They agreed further that they would share control, with Arthur having it when things were quiet, Ragen when danger threatened. But this was much more easily agreed to than carried out. During the next seven years the multitude of personalities, including Ragen, seemed much more out on their own than under any control by Arthur. Allen, Tommy and Danny painted tirelessly—portraits, landscapes and still lifes, respectively—and sold their work through a flower shop where Allen worked for a while. But "for a while" was the keynote of Allen's work history. The many jobs he managed to get were menial—Arthur disdainfully labeled them "bloody slave work"—and brief, since there were so many mischievous cooks to spoil the broth. His, or their, erratic job performance made it impossible for him to keep any job for any respectable length of time. Even the Navy gave up on him after only six weeks, releasing him with an honorable discharge after a puzzled navy psychiatrist reported that he was "temperamentally unsuited for further training."

He, or they, did some traveling. Although Allen had entered the Navy, it was Phil who left it and who went off on a jaunt to New York City instead of going home to Columbus. After a couple of days there Phil gave way to David, whose chief contribution to the tour was to lose the community duffle bag, simply leaving it on a sidewalk because it was too heavy to lug around. He soon gave way to Allen, who at first assumed he must be in Chicago waiting for a flight to Columbus. He discovered otherwise when he got to the airport. Although he was four days late for his flight to Columbus, he managed to fast-talk his way home on another plane. On a similar occasion a year or so later he unexpectedly found himself in London, where he cut short Arthur's visit with a panicky flight back home.

His work experience—he was usually the one who found the jobs for the others to lose—was so depressing and unprofitable that Ragen and Phil and a couple of the minor, less savory personalities resorted to extracurricular activities that in March, 1975, earned Milligan a conviction for robbery and a two-year stay in an Ohio prison. After his parole in April, 1977, he drifted about the Columbus area and in and out of various jobs until Ragen took over, determined to do something about the financial situation. What he did was to rob the three women from the Ohio State University area in October, 1977. The rape, and the attempted rape, was done by Adalana—who one night also shaved off his moustache.

Milligan's post-conviction therapy under Dr. Caul's direction at the Athens mental health center was showing great promise until the end of March, 1979, when the Columbus *Dispatch* banner-headlined a report that he was being "allowed to roam free and unsupervised" in the town of Athens. This was the beginning of a series of such stories, in the *Dispatch* and other papers, as well as editorials on such topics as "Legislation Needed to Protect Society." A couple of state politicians joined the chorus, which soon grew so loud that Dr. Caul and the center's superintendent felt compelled to ask Milligan to forego his unattended leaves until the storm blew over. Milligan, deeply hurt that his good behavior had netted him public distrust and obloquy, came apart. He became violent and was given Thorazine to calm him. Thorazine, however, for all its effectiveness in treating schizophrenia, can aggravate hysterical dissociation, and that is what it did. Within a week or so Milligan was in a cell in the locked ward raving like a madman, his personalities coming and going rapidly, completely out of control.

Although the public uproar continued—even the local chapter of the National Organization for Women got into the act, charging that Dr. Caul's program of therapy showed "a deliberate and flagrant disregard for the safety of women in the surrounding communities"—Milligan was kept at the Athens hospital, chiefly on the recommendation of Cornelia Wilbur. His condition began improving again. Some of the townspeople treated him sympathetically. University students regularly greeted him in a friendly way. Some of his paintings were put on display in a local bank. He conducted himself well during a couple of gentle television interviews. But then one morning, while out jogging near the hospital grounds, he was stalked by a couple of men in an automobile. When it stopped, a window was rolled down, a gun appeared, and a voice yelled "Milligan!" As Ragen dived for cover, two ill-aimed shots rang out, and the car sped away. The fragile Milligan had come apart again.

The violence resumed, and in October, 1979, Milligan was sent by court order to the state hospital for the criminally insane in Lima, where the officials rejected the notion of multiple personality and ordered that he be treated with Stelazine, another antipsychotic drug known to aggravate hysterical dissociation. Subsequently in an "altercation with an attendant," he was severely beaten. And not long after this Daniel Keyes, who was not allowed to visit him at Lima, received several letters from several of the personalities, one written in Serbo-Croatian and another in Arabic, reporting essentially that Billy was now permanently asleep and that Ragen was holding the fort as best he could.

In November, 1980, after the Lima facility had been changed in function from a hospital to a prison, Milligan was sent to the maximum-security Dayton Forensic Center. In April, 1981, a state appellate court ruled that his rights had been violated when he was sent to Lima but approved his being kept at the Dayton facility because of the danger he presented to himself and others. Not long thereafter, during a visit, Keyes asked Milligan which personality he was talking to. Milligan answered that he no longer knew. He seemed very, very tired. When Keyes asked him if he knew where he was, he responded that David had a name for it. He called it "The Dying Place."

Bibliography

Allen, Clifford. *Modern Discoveries in Medical Psychology.* New York: Macmillan, 1962.

Allison, Ralph B. "A New Treatment Approach for Multiple Personalities." *American Journal of Clinical Hypnosis,* 1974, pp. 15 ff.

_____, and Ted Schwarz. *Minds in Many Pieces: The Making of a Very Special Doctor.* New York: Rawson, Wade, 1980.

American Psychiatric Association. *Diagnostic and Statistical Manual of Mental Disorders.* Washington, D.C.: The Association, 1980.

Beahrs, John O. *Unity and Multiplicity: Multilevel Consciousness of Self in Hypnosis, Psychiatric Disorder and Mental Health.* New York: Brunner/Mazel, 1982.

Boor, Myron. 'The Multiple Personality Epidemic: Additional Cases and Inferences Regarding Diagnosis, Etiology, Dynamics, and Treatment." *Journal of Nervous and Mental Disorders,* May 1982, pp. 302-4.

Brandsma, Jeffrey M., and Arnold M. Ludwig. "A Case of Multiple Personality: Diagnosis and Therapy." *The International Journal of Clinical and Experimental Hypnosis,* 1974, pp. 216-33.

Cherry, Laurence. "Multiple Personalities." *Glamour,* August 1980, pp. 218 ff.

Coles, Robert. "Arthur, Ragen, Allen et Al." *The New York Times Book Review,* Nov. 15, 1981, pp. 9 f.

Coons, Philip M. "Multiple Personality: Diagnostic Considerations." *Journal of Clinical Psychiatry,* October 1980, pp. 330-6.

Cory, Charles E. "A Divided Self." *Journal of Abnormal Psychology,* 1919, pp. 281-5.

____. "Patience Worth." *Psychological Review,* 1919, pp. 397-406.

Cutten, G.B. "The Case of John Kinsel." *Psychological Review,* 1903, pp. 465-97, 615-32.

157

Cutler, B., and J. Reed. "Multiple Personality." *Psychological Medicine*, 1975, pp. 18 ff.

Dana, C.L. "Mrs. S." *Psychological Review*, 1894, pp. 570-80.

Ellenberger, Henri F. *The Discovery of the Unconscious*. New York: Basic Books, 1970.

Flournoy, T. *De Indes à la Planète Mars: Étude sur un Cas de Somnambulisme avec Glossalalie.* Geneva, 1899.

Footlick, Jerrold K. "The Ten Faces of Billy." *Newsweek*, Dec. 18, 1978, p. 106.

Gilbert, J.A. "X." *New York Medical Record*, 1902, pp. 207-11.

Gordon, Jesse E. *Patterns of Behavior.* New York: Macmillan, 1963.

Greaves, G. "Multiple Personality 165 Years After Mary Reynolds." *Journal of Nervous and Mental Disorders*, 1980, pp. 577 ff.

Hale, N.G. *Morton Prince: Psychotherapy and Multiple Personality, Selected Essays.* Cambridge, Mass.: Harvard University Press, 1975.

Hawksworth, Henry, with Ted Schwarz. *The Five of Me.* Chicago: Henry Regnery, 1977.

Hilgard, E.R. "Dissociation Revisited." In M. Henle, J. Jayner and J. Sullivan, *Contributions to the History of Psychology* (New York: Springer, 1973).

_____. *Divided Consciousness: Multiple Controls in Human Thought and Action.* New York: John Wiley & Sons, 1977.

Horton, Paul, and Derek Miller. "The Etiology of Multiple Personality." *Comprehensive Psychiatry*, March 1972, pp. 151-9.

James, William. *The Principles of Psychology.* New York: Holt, 1890.

Janet, Pierre. *The Major Symptoms of Hysteria.* New York: Macmillan, 1907.

Keerdoja, Eileen. "Treating the 24 Faces of Billy." *Newsweek*, Aug. 21, 1981, pp. 20 f.

Keyes, Daniel. *The Minds of Billy Milligan.* New York: Random House, 1981.

Lester, David. "Multiple Personality: A Review." *Psychology*, February 1977, pp. 54-9.

Ludwig, Arnold M.; Jeffrey M. Brandsma, Cornelia Wilbur, Fernando Bendfeldt and Douglas Jameson. "The Objective Study of a Multiple Personality: or, Are Four Heads Better Than One?" *Archives of General Psychiatry*, April 1972, pp. 298-310.

McDougall, William. *An Outline of Abnormal Psychology.* London: Methuen, 1926.

McKellar, Peter. *Mindsplit: The Psychology of Multiple Personality and Dissociated Self.* London: J.M. Dent & Sons, 1979.

"The Man with Ten Personalities." *Time,* Oct. 23, 1978, p. 102.

Mason, R.O. "Alma Z." *Journal of Nervous and Mental Disorders,* 1893, pp. 420-23.

Mayer, Edward E. "A Case of Localized Amnesia." *Journal of the American Medical Association,* 1901, pp. 1601-5.

Muhl, Anita. "Automatic Writing as an Indicator of the Fundamental Factors Underlying the Personality." *Journal of Abnormal Psychology,* 1922, pp. 168 ff.

Murphy, Gardner. *An Outline of Abnormal Psychology.* New York: Modern Library, 1929.

_____. *Personality.* New York: Harper & Row, 1947.

Osborne, A.E. "The Tinsmith." *The Medico-Legal Journal,* 1894, pp. 22-41.

Prince, Morton. *The Dissociation of a Personality: A Biographical Study in Abnormal Psychology.* New York: Longman, Greens, 1905.

Rapaport, David. *Emotions and Memory.* New York: International Universities Press, 1959.

Rigall, Robert M. "A Case of Multiple Personality." *The Lancet,* 1931, pp. 846-8.

Robinson, E.S., and F. Richardson-Robinson (eds.). *Readings in General Psychology.* Chicago: University of Chicago Press, 1929.

Rosenbaum, Milton. "The Role of the Term 'Schizophrenia' in the Diagnosis of Multiple Personality." *Archives of General Psychiatry,* December 1980, pp. 1383-5.

Schreiber, Flora Rheta. *Sybil.* Chicago: Henry Regnery Co., 1973.

Sidis, Boris, and Simon P. Goodhart. *Multiple Personality: An Experimental Investigation into the Nature of Human Individuality.* New York: Appleton, 1905.

Stoller, Robert J. *Splitting: A Case of Female Masculinity.* New York: New York Times Book Co., 1973.

Taylor, W.S., and Mabel F. Martin. "Multiple Personality." *Journal of Abnormal and Social Psychology,* 1944, pp. 281-300.

Thigpen, Corbett H., and Hervey M. Cleckley. "A Case of Multiple Personality." *Journal of Abnormal and Social Psychology,* 1954, pp. 135-51.

_____, and _____. *The Three Faces of Eve.* New York: McGraw-Hill, 1957.

White, Robert Winthrop. *The Abnormal Personality: A Textbook.* New York: Ronald Press, 1956.

Wholey, Cornelius C. "A Case of Multiple Personality." *American Journal of Psychiatry*, January 1933, pp. 653-87.

Index

161